Advance Praise for *An Improb*

"Charles Lubar's life story reads lik[...] is true of his amazing career, his encounters, his very acute description of a very intricate world. For his first book, Lubar knows how to propose a 'page-turner.' A must-read!"

—**Philippe Labro**, French Author, Journalist, Film Director, and Television Host

"Over twenty plus years, Chuck has been an invaluable advisor to my family and was instrumental in setting up a structure that will benefit generations to come. His advice, both personal and professional as we negotiated some very complex family issues, was critical in the eventual stabilization of our circumstances and a solid foundation on which to preserve my father and grandfather's hard-earned wealth."

—**Peter Livanos**, Greek Shipping Family

"No one could restore John to the UK until we met Charles Lubar. No one. Chuck is the savior and hero who got John Barry back to his beloved country of birth."

—**Laurie Barry**, Wife of World-Famous Film Composer John Barry

"Charles Lubar's *An Improbable Journey* offers a candid and entertaining look at the world of an international attorney who spent over forty years offering financial and personal advice to Americans living abroad. His spellbinding anecdotes give a unique insight into the lives of his many famous clients, but also reveal the warmth and empathy that made the author into a trusted advisor of legendary stature."

—**Michael Haggiag**, Film and Television Producer

AN
Improbable
Journey

MUSIC, MONEY, *and the* LAW

CHARLES G. LUBAR

Post Hill
PRESS

A POST HILL PRESS BOOK
ISBN: 978-1-63758-552-8
ISBN (eBook): 978-1-63758-553-5

An Improbable Journey:
Music, Money, and the Law
© 2023 by Charles G. Lubar
All Rights Reserved

Cover Design by Conroy Accord
Cover Photo by Josephine Ettinger, LaLuna Photography
Interior Design by Yoni Limor

Post Hill Press
New York • Nashville
posthillpress.com

Published in the United States of America
1 2 3 4 5 6 7 8 9 10

*For my wife, Dominique, whom I met
in 1975, not long after I set up my
own practice in London, and who has
supported me and seen me through
almost all of the stories that make up this
book, sometimes even with her valuable
critical eye.*

TABLE OF CONTENTS

INTRODUCTION
On the Concorde with Michael Jackson 11

CHAPTER ONE
Where to Begin? 15

CHAPTER TWO
"Bond...James Bond" 57

CHAPTER THREE
East Germany, Here I Come 77

CHAPTER FOUR
Miss Piggy Comes On to Kris Kristofferson
and Other Muppet Tales 109

CHAPTER FIVE
The Linda Lovelace, Chuck Traynor,
Marilyn Chambers Triumvirate 129

CHAPTER SIX
Michael Jackson Has a Case of Beatlemania 147

CHAPTER SEVEN
Coke Dinner 159

CHAPTER EIGHT
Oh, the People, the Stories 171

CHAPTER NINE
An Economic Benedict Arnold: on Expatriation ... 197
CHAPTER TEN
Risk/Reward 207

BIBLIOGRAPHICAL NOTES............... 215
ACKNOWLEDGMENTS 217
ABOUT THE AUTHOR.................. 223

There was a very cautious man,
Who never laughed or played.
He never risked,
He never tried,
He never sang or prayed.
And when he one day passed away,
His insurance was denied.
For since he never really lived,
They claimed he never died.

—Anonymous

On the Concorde with Michael Jackson

One morning, I was flying aboard the Concorde from London to New York, and I noticed that Michael Jackson—yes, *the* Michael Jackson—was seated far up toward the nose of the plane. Seated beside Michael, necessarily, was a massive bodyguard. I, meanwhile, was seated some several rows back from the King of Pop beside an amiable man who happened to be one of my best clients.

"Would you like a Concorde menu signed by Michael Jackson for your son?" I said to my client.

Indeed, he did. But he wondered how I could ever get an autograph from the highly protected star.

Without giving him an answer, I stood up and went to the very front of the plane and leaned over to Michael—honestly, I wasn't sure whether I was about to get hit right in the face by the bodyguard—and said, "Michael, you may not remember me, but I was your tax lawyer on the acquisition of the ATV Music catalogue."

The ATV Music catalogue, you might recall, included all those ever-valuable Beatles publishing copyrights.

Michael said that of course he remembered me, and he greeted me kindly. And why shouldn't Michael have remembered me? The fact was, back in the mid-1980s, I had contributed to making him a lot of money on a deal for the ages.

"I'm sitting with a client a few rows back, and I would really appreciate it if you were willing to sign your autograph on a Concorde menu that my client could give to his son."

Michael was very affable, very friendly, and he signed his name to the menu. I returned to my client, not a little bit excited to have been remembered by the King of Pop and with a token in my hand bearing his signature.

CHAPTER ONE
Where to Begin?

In October of 2000, I was asked back to Harvard Law School, my alma mater, to speak at the Traphagen Distinguished Alumni Speaker Series. Why had I been invited? Well, in some sense, I suppose that's for the reader to decide. But I treated it as an honor and also as something of a duty to talk about my career path and how it was different from the type of career one would normally expect of a person coming out of an educational background like Yale and Harvard Law School, much less with a master's degree in taxation and three years with the Chief Counsel's Office of the IRS. My honor stated:

Charles G. Lubar '66

Eminent international attorney, trusted counselor to Les Stars, tax practitioner extraordinaire, successful son of Harvard; with vision and force, you advanced the multinational practice of Morgan, Lewis, rendering it a formidable global law firm.

Attest:

Robert C. Clark
Dean of the Faculty of Law
October 10, 2000

In lecturing to the students about my career, I felt some obligation to talk about my rather unusual path and how it had nevertheless brought me to a point where a dean of Harvard Law School would think it worth engaging me to discuss my life with an audience of future lawyers. Moreover, for the reader to grasp my message, I think it would be helpful to say something about my conventional life first—that is, the life I had lived up until I decided to take a great leap of faith and depart the IRS for a highly risky business venture in Nairobi, Kenya, in 1969. And so right here, as with those Harvard Law students back on that autumn day in the year 2000, I will start my story at the beginning.

Early Life

My parents came from a conventional, albeit liberal, upper-middle-class Jewish family. My father was a practicing lawyer turned something of a real estate entrepreneur over the course of his career, and my mother worked for the Procurement Division of the US Government for a number of years until she married my father. I was the oldest of three children, with two younger sisters. Washington, DC, was my hometown, Davenport Street and Connecticut Avenue, NW, on the way to Chevy Chase Circle, a comfortable part of the world to come of age. At fourteen, on Christmas holiday at the Kenilworth Lodge in Sebring, Florida, I would find my first calling: golf. My father was a decent golfer, and he thought that I should give the sport a try. So for one week, a local pro named Joe Circella taught me how to swing a golf club, and I took to it so naturally that I actually broke 90 before leaving Kenilworth Lodge. Back home, Jack Garvin, the assistant pro at the Woodmont Country Club in suburban Maryland where my father was a member, suggested that I join the Junior Golf Program in DC, which was run by a USGA official, Frank Emmet. Emmet had developed junior golf programs all over the United States. And so began quite a successful junior golf career of competitive tournaments in Washington and throughout the country.

I played first in the fifteen-and-under competitions in the DC area program and won my share of tournaments over my years as a junior golfer (under eighteen). I was also runner-up in the Club Championship at Woodmont Country Club, Medal Play Club Champion a few years later, and Junior Club Champion for several years running. Nationally, I played in the National Junior Tournaments in Bethesda, Maryland and Minneapolis, Minnesota; and the International Junior Chamber of Commerce tournaments in Columbus, Ohio and Tucson, Arizona. My most significant success was in winning the Washington Metropolitan Area Schoolboy Championship in 1958 in my junior year in high school by the biggest margin in the history of the tournament. I also had the distinction of having my name in headlines in the local Washington newspaper when I lost in the third round of the National Junior at Manor Country Club in Maryland along with Jack Nicklaus. The headline simply read: "Lubar, Nicklaus lose in Junior Golf."

One item of note. In my competitive junior golf career, I often played at various golf courses that were very restricted in their memberships, most likely no Jews or Blacks allowed, and sometimes even no Catholics. In one particular case, Frank Emmet noted to me that one club, Chevy Chase, where we played some important matches, not only didn't permit Jewish members, they didn't even permit Jewish guests. I did take this personally, and I do remember taking a towel from the locker room, monogrammed Chevy Chase Club, and kept it as a memento for years. This sensitivity led me to notice that throughout my junior golf career that there were never any Black players in any of the tournaments. I raised this a couple of years after I graduated in the context of issuing invitations for the Bobby Gorin Invitational, an important junior golf tournament named after a close friend of mine who had been killed in a car accident two years before. I discussed this with Frank Emmet, and he agreed that if I could identify some qualified Black golfers in the high school programs in Washington, he would ensure they would be invited. I contacted the athletic department of Cardozo High School and the director of athletics, Frank Bolden, who did identify two brothers who were good golfers, and both were issued invitations to the Bobby Gorin Invitational the following year. This was the beginning of Black participation in the Washington Metropolitan Area competitive golf program, and I received a personal thank you letter from Frank Bolden on behalf of the Cardozo athletic family for "your very wonderful sense of sportsmanship and fair play in sponsoring the two Brockington brothers in the recent Bobby Gorin Invitational."

But if I wasn't holding a golf club, I could very likely be found with a guitar in my hands. As a child, I had played the piano, but after four years, I'd come to dislike the instrument so much that I wanted nothing more to do with it. My mother agreed to let me stop with the piano, but she would not abide the end of my musical journey. She sat me down, aged fourteen—and I'll never forget, I even remember the chair she sat me down in—and she said, "Okay, son, pick an instrument."

I had no idea which I would choose. Would it be a slide trombone or perhaps the trumpet? I knew I didn't like playing so many chords on the piano and that I was much more interested in the treble and the melody, and I thought if I learned the guitar these issues would be resolved. I was dead wrong—and yet I was not discouraged. I loved the guitar immediately. I have no doubt that the instrument has taught me much about trusting my gut and going on feel, for that's what it took to make me a reasonably good guitarist. To that point, I must also credit one of my early teachers, one of the great jazz guitarists of the twentieth century, Charlie Byrd. I was the last pupil Charlie Byrd ever had. One day, at the end of a lesson he turned to me and said:

"Chuck, I can't teach you anymore. I've got a new gig."

It was the Showboat Lounge in Washington, DC, which, in fact, would launch his career.

I thanked him for what he'd taught me about the guitar. But I would have an opportunity to thank him again thirty years later when I attended a concert at the Royal Albert Hall in London. He was on a European tour with two other jazz guitar greats, Herb Ellis and Barney Kessel. I went up to him following his performance and said, "Mister Byrd, you probably don't remember me, but I was your last pupil, Chuck Lubar." Wouldn't you know it, he *did* remember me.

In my years in high school, I began to play the guitar and sing with a group of young musicians. We were called the Collegians, and we covered lots of early rock 'n' roll, from Chuck Berry to Little Richard, Buddy Holly to Elvis, enjoying ourselves with the "teeny boppers" of the time. The best part of this early experience was that it gave me a pretty good sense of stage presence, some modest confidence in my ability—or at least willingness to perform live—and certainly provided me inspiration for the creation of a really skilled band during my time upcoming at Yale. Indeed, when I first arrived on the Yale campus in 1959, I wondered whether it might not be possible to create a rock 'n' roll band that played much of the music I had been playing in high school with the Collegians. I advertised on campus for a variety of different musicians, interviewed potential participants, auditioned them on their respective instruments, and put together a superb group of multi-talented and diverse characters from all parts of the country. On drums was Steven MacKinnon, who played in the Thunderbirds for our first year (but not again until our fifty-year Yale reunion when we put the band together for a final time; Bob Buchanan, class of '64, was our drummer for the last three years). On bass, I had a three-hundred-pound sensation from Cincinnati named Scrib Mantle. On sax, Rich Samuels, from Chicago, a great blues saxophonist. On lead guitar, Billy Kramer from Dallas, Texas, who could throw the guitar over his head and play solos (and remains a good friend to this day), and then the final addition to the band, probably the most natural musician of us all, Geoff Noyes, on fiddle, harmonica, and blues piano. I sang and played rhythm guitar and, as the Thunderbirds, we made a big name for ourselves not just in New Haven but up and down the eastern seaboard playing for fraternity parties, women's college events, and Yale residential and other college parties. Our repertoire consisted of the rock 'n' roll world I described above, but in addition, we added lots of down-home Southern blues, including Jimmy Reed, John Lee Hooker, and North Carolina band the Hot Nuts. Much of our repertoire stayed with me for years, and through my life, I would often harken back to that amazing body of musicians I put together our on our freshman campus in 1959.

But the confidence I showed in putting together the Thunderbirds did not tell the whole story, for when I went off to Yale, in the fall of 1959, I was a bit intimidated. Like so many kids from public high schools upon arriving at a school like Yale and finding oneself surrounded by so many students who had had much better high school educations, having attended some of the finest prep schools in the world, like Andover, Exeter, and Lawrenceville, I worried about my academic readiness. What I didn't realize was that the public-school kids were at least as smart as those that were privately educated and were actually as well-prepared as anyone. After a year on campus, I figured out how this new world worked. I came out of the first and second semesters in the top 10 percent of the class, and then I qualified as number one on the freshman golf team; and along with the Thunderbirds, I was doing quite well in my new surroundings. Even my two Catholic football player roommates from the South Side of Chicago, who had categorized me as a narrow intellectual upon our first introductions, came to respect me. (I came to respect them, too, and one, Lee March, even became a lifelong friend.) My golf career at Yale was modestly successful, although I played my best golf in my years as captain of the freshman team and my first year on the varsity. There were five of us who played together for all four years, were all good friends, and were about equal in ability and success on the team. I ended my career at Yale with a record of twenty-nine wins and six losses but have played only a limited amount of golf since that time and certainly almost no competitive golf.

I had one tragedy in my four years at Yale. My father, who had been a profound influence on my life, died suddenly of a massive heart attack a month before his fifty-second birthday. I was a junior and just twenty. He had been an inveterate smoker—three packs a day—and in his final year, he used to feed an ulcer with scotch and milk. As an immediate consequence, I never touched a cigarette and kept an almost cream-free diet the rest of my life. Comforting my mother and two sisters and living through the consequences of his death almost resulted in my having to leave Yale for a semester. But my mother insisted I stay, and I ended up only dropping one class and making it up with summer school. Nonetheless, my father's death affected me profoundly. I had lost my mentor, my consistent encourager, and my strength. I had my many youthful successes, but always with the support of my father and mother. Now I certainly had a sense of vulnerability and loneliness I never realized I had before. There was a sense that I was now on my own and, despite my mother's continued support, life's decisions became suddenly my own.

My years at Yale were otherwise very satisfying, and I graduated magna cum laude. But at that time, after finishing with one's undergraduate studies, if further education was the goal, one tended to go straight into the next levels of education with no "gap" years or work experience in the "real" world. And that's how in the fall of 1963, I found myself a student at Harvard Law School now studying to be a lawyer. I had received good advice from my father that a legal training was an excellent training for life, and this very likely influenced my decision to go off to Cambridge in the first place. My father was also very sensitive to the fact that he had never learned anything about taxation. When he had been at law school in the 1930s, taxation wasn't even a profession demanding legal qualifications. Therefore, in addition to suggesting that it would be a good idea to go to law school, my father also said it would be smart to learn something about taxation. To his everlasting credit, my father never put pressure on me to be a lawyer or to study taxation. With his encouragement and his light touch, he let me decide on my own that both were something worth studying. And it worked. Without any second guessing, I went off to law school thinking that I really wanted that legal education no matter what the future held for me. Likewise, I took a lot of tax courses at Harvard, knowing it would be important to have some knowledge in this area of the law.

I had a decent record at Harvard Law School. I didn't drive myself as I could have—no part of me could have fathomed being asked back to the school some forty years later to lecture students on my career, no—but I got a first-class legal education.

In retrospect, my only real accomplishment at Harvard Law School was my world-wind romance with my first wife, Nancy, and our marriage in Dallas, Texas about a month after I graduated. She was a fascinating young woman, a graduate of Mount Holyoke College, who left her Dallas family and was teaching in the poverty program in Boston. Of course, I was too young to marry, having never yet seen the reality of the world around me. I had been cocooned in my sheltered educational experience. Our marriage was destined to fail and it ultimately did so, but not before the birth of our daughter, Katherine, in Washington, D.C. Katherine would eventually move back to Dallas after my separation from her mother in London. This was a very painful time of my life. I felt the separation from my daughter powerfully. Nancy really wanted to go back to Dallas, and the English courts almost always ordered "care and control" of a young minor (Katherine was barely seven) to the mother. Although I did have calls periodically and engineered my travel as best I could to get to Dallas, there was no internet in those days nor video conferencing, so communication was difficult and expensive. Ultimately, when she was twenty-four, Katherine came back to London to live, and she is now an accomplished modern artist settled in London.

But let's return to my life after graduation from law school.

Next, I had to decide what I was going to do with my career. I never bothered to interview at all with the big law firms, for after my father's passing and with his small law practice still a successful operation, I thought I would just return to Washington and take a position there. Truth be told, I had no idea what that would even mean. What would practicing law at my father's old firm entail? What kinds of cases would I take on? What I learned quite soon after my arrival there was that the firm was nothing like it had been when my father was alive. My father was a very entrepreneurial lawyer, and when he passed away, the entrepreneurial spirit of the firm passed along with him. All the same, I went there to learn something about the practice of law. And while doing so, I decided to get a master's degree in taxation from Georgetown University. From classes I'd taken in taxation at Harvard, I knew that I liked the subject. Even before then, as a high school student writing a paper on the Sixteenth Amendment, from which the tax code derived, I had a real scholarly interest in the subject and also a fascination with the intricacies of tax law. I did well in the master's degree program, and by that time, I realized that there was no future staying with the small group of lawyers at my father's old firm. I also sensed that I wanted to become a tax lawyer. Though I had no real understanding of how one went about becoming a tax lawyer, I did have one great advantage: as a result of my active competitive life as a junior golfer, I had gotten to know a number of the golfers at Woodmont Country Club. Several turned out to be successful tax lawyers in Washington, and they were only too happy to give me advice on a career path. Three of these successful lawyers gave me the same advice: work for the government first, and in the order of priority choose the Chief Counsel's Office of the IRS, the Appellate Tax Division of the Department of Justice, or a Tax Court clerkship. This was crucial information, and I was fortunate to have it.

I went to the Chief Counsel's Office first. They had a number of divisions there, but the one that interested me most was the Interpretative Division, which was really the think-tank of the IRS. Their focus was on analyzing and problem solving when questions arose from any IRS office in the United States. Quite literally, an IRS agent would have an issue and would send the matter to the Interpretative Division of the Chief Counsel's Office for review. The division was not an advocate for the IRS, nor was it representing the IRS. The job was to come up with the right answer. The IRS seniors might not always like the conclusions reached by the division, and they might make suggestions to Congress to change the law, but it was a purist kind of job—and that appealed to me. I asked about availability in the division, and sure enough, they were prepared to hire me. Being offered such a senior position as a young lawyer, I had to make a four-year commitment, and I agreed to do so.

The IRS

During my years in the Chief Counsel's Office, I learned so much and was absolutely fascinated by the job. For starters, I found out what it was to be a tax lawyer and about the kind of problems one faced in the practice of law. I got to familiarize myself with every type of problem-solving issue that you could come across in the field. I saw corporate transactions, life insurance problems, pension problems, charitable issues, trust and estate issues, and oddball individual cases. I was part of a team that looked at the taxation of Lloyd's of London, the big insurance group in the UK that was expanding its business in the United States. Lloyd's of London had gone in to the IRS for a very narrow ruling on the taxation of their interest income on their New York accounts with Citibank. The IRS was not pleased with what they saw, since twenty-five years earlier they had ruled that Lloyd's was not "engaged in a trade or business" in the US. So, what did the IRS do in such a situation? They had us rip apart the Lloyd's tax position and reconstitute it. Normally, you had a whole body of law on the taxation of insurance companies. But this was a much more complicated situation because Lloyd's at that time was a group of individual entrepreneurial insurers—4,500 individual insurers to be exact. That sort of constitution didn't work so well under the Internal Revenue Code, because all of the tax rules on insurance businesses applied only to companies and not to individuals. I spent a good portion of time trying to unravel this very unusual structure and then piece it back together. For me, this was my first exposure to international tax law. What it taught me, first of all, was that the laws of developed countries could be very divergent in analyzing tax issues. For example, some tax systems were on an "accrual" basis, some on a "cash" basis; the UK had a special regime for insurance businesses like Lloyd's, but the US had special rules only for insurance companies—not individuals— carrying on an insurance business. Some tax regimes taxed income only from local sources, others taxed worldwide income. Some gave credit for foreign taxes paid, others only gave deductions. Moreover, the tolerance for tax planning and aggressive tax structuring was very different from one country to the next. In any event, we resolved the complexities of the taxation of Lloyd's of London, but not without help from the Treasury Secretary's Office in both jurisdictions, not just the tax authorities. My learning curve in this experience was enormous. One attractive element, however, was that because of the nature of the office, I wasn't under time-pressure to get a brief out the next day, and I never had a client on my back. I could take the time to learn about a particular tax issue and offer my view of the "correct" answer. It was a remarkable experience, one that prepared me for so much that was to follow.

Was I a Spy?

In 1964, I took my first trip to Russia. I had studied Russian all four years at Yale. People have asked me why I did so. The answer? Sputnik. In 1957, when Sputnik went up into orbit, the first satellite of its kind to do so, it looked to me like Russian was going to be the language of the future. Therefore, why not learn the language? I actually found Russian relatively easy, and I did very well. Why I ever took this trip in the first place was owed in part to my study of the language.

In those days, to travel through Russia as an American, you had to go with a guide from Intourist, the government travel agency. But the Russian government had loosened up to a point that it was no longer risky for Russians to talk to foreigners, which I did quite extensively, even going on occasion to the homes of some of the locals and listening to stories about their lives.

One day, I split off from my tourist guide and wandered the streets of Moscow on my own. I happened to be carrying a guitar with me that day, and I ran across a very attractive young woman. I didn't believe that she had been following me. (Perhaps *I* had been following her.) But we struck up a conversation, and I said, "Well, would you like me to play some folk songs for you? Maybe we could go into Gorky Park together."

And she said, "What a great idea."

Off we went into Gorky Park, and we sat down on a bench. I started to strum the instrument and we were having a lovely time, whereby all of a sudden, two Russian police came charging directly at us and began shouting at me in such a way that convinced me that I was in serious trouble. But then the woman with whom I had been sitting stood up and started barking back at the policemen. My knowledge of the Russian language was not so advanced that I could understand what she was saying. However, I could see that the police were duly frightened, and they backed away, leaving us. A little bell then rang off in my head, and I remembered that in discussing trips to Russia with various people I knew who had traveled to the country, I had come to understand that Russians loved to compromise foreigners, especially in their hotel rooms, and that they were particularly adept at taking photographs or video in a clandestine manner, betting that some of these Americans would be bribable or subject to extortion some years down the line. I said to myself, "You have to turn down this opportunity," and I simply played my songs and off I went in my own separate direction. These were the times—the Cold War at its heights—and you had to think and make decisions accordingly.

Some four years later, in the summer of 1968, not much at all had changed in the Communist world. My wife and I took a trip down the Danube, from Vienna to Budapest, and about a month after returning home to Washington, DC, I received a phone call at my desk at the IRS:

> **"Mister Lubar, this is Agent X from the FBI. My partner and I would like to come talk to you and your wife this weekend out at your home in Maryland."**

Though surprised by the caller, I said, "Sure. Why not."

That Saturday morning, I met with two very characteristic FBI agents: trench coats, hats, one tall and easygoing, one short and tough-natured. I had no idea what they could possibly want with me.

They said, "Mister Lubar, have you ever been to Budapest?"

"Yes, sure," I said. "I just recently went down the Danube with my wife, from Vienna to Budapest."

"Yes, well, since you've been back, have you been contacted by any Hungarians or any people from the Eastern European émigré community?"

I said, "What? You've come all the way out to Maryland to ask me if I've been approached by Hungarian emigrants? Why would you do that?"

"Because we are interested in whether you had contact."

"Well, the is answer is *no*, absolutely not," I said. "I did not have any contacts whatsoever. But let *me* ask you *this*: what about the five or six times I've been in the Soviet Embassy? You do know about that, don't you?"

Whereupon the two agents looked at one another, completely baffled. They had absolutely no knowledge of this detail of my life. But I had been in a diplomatic program for a period of time involved in running a young adults' program for diplomats. Historically, the Russian diplomats had never participated in this or any of the programs. But more recently, the Russians had opened up and allowed their diplomats to participate. The program was completely innocuous. We gave them introductions to Washington, DC and mixed with the young diplomatic community. But this had brought me inside the Russian Embassy on numerous occasions. Sometimes they had events, such as cocktail parties and film screenings.

One FBI agent said, "Well, do you remember the names of the people you've met in this capacity?"

"Sure," I said, "I know them all—" and I reeled off a half-dozen names.

They asked that we go through the list of names carefully. I gave them the first name and they said:

"Oh, yes, we know him. He's a cultural attaché at the embassy. He's very interested in the arts. He's a good person."

I gave them a second name.

"Oh, *yes*, him—he's not with the embassy. He's with a trade delegation, independent of the embassy. He's clean."

"What about *this* man?" I said, naming another name.

"Indeed, he's the first secretary of the economic division. He's a scholarly guy, and he's a professional diplomat. We know him."

"And how about *this* fellow?" I said, naming yet another person I had met while in the young diplomats program.

"Yes, we know him, too. We know him *very* well. Among other things, *he* is a member of the KGB, and he has responsibility for watching out for all émigrés from Eastern Europe."

I said, "*Oh?* Okay. And how do you know all of this?"

"Because it's our job to know," they said.

"And why do you want to quiz me about it?"

They pointed out that I worked for the Chief Counsel's Office of the IRS, and because of this, the Russians had an interest in me.

"In *me?*"

"Yes."

"Why would they care about me?"

The FBI agents began to explain that the Russians viewed the IRS as a super-human organism, one capable of finding anyone in the United States if they put their minds and their technology to it.

"And we have a big problem with that, because in the United States, there are a reasonable number of what we call 'illegals.' You remember Colonel

Rudolf Abel. He was exchanged for Gary Powers, after Gary Powers was shot down in his plane."

I said, "Yes, I remember that."

"Yes, well, Colonel Rudolf Abel was in fact one of these so-called 'illegals.' The 'illegals' are Russians who are trained *in* Russia to be Americans."

As it were, there were a couple of walled-off, fabricated cities that existed in Russia that looked like Main Street, USA; and in these "cities," these "illegals" were taught to speak English *as* an American, learned the history of the country, and about things such as sports and entertainment, and were trained to act as if they *were* Americans. The Russian government would then plant these people in select parts of the United States with all sorts of fake papers, sometimes fake jobs. Many of them were scientifically trained. The Russians hoped that at some point, these people would integrate into American life well enough so that they would have something to report back to the Russian government about everything and anything. However, the Russians were scared to death of the IRS because they believed that the IRS knew how to identify and locate these individuals. The Russians did whatever they could to make sure that these people were protected, between false papers regarding citizenship and birth certificates. One was described to me as having come from Duluth, Minnesota from a church that had burned down, this "illegal" carrying a birth certificate from someone who had perished in the fire.

"Anyway, Mister Lubar," said the FBI agents, "we think you can help us."

"You think *I* can help you?"

"Yes. If you just told us when you met people and what you discussed in the course of those meetings, if you just repeated it all back to us—we'll pay for these lunches and dinners, and your information gathering will feed into our knowledge bank, and maybe someday it will be helpful."

"You think so?"

"Yes," said the FBI agents.

So, I agreed to it.

I played this role of the informant for a year and a half, and it was fascinating. I didn't know if I was being a traitor to the foreigners that I was meeting or if I was being a good citizen to the country, providing the FBI with information about Russians with whom they were concerned. I wasn't apprehensive, though perhaps I should have been, given the circumstances. In fact, I was fairly relaxed. Sure enough, I told these agents about all the people that I met. One time, when I met "D" and asked him what he was doing for the weekend, he replied that he was going out to West Virginia with his wife and family, that they were going to visit the Appalachian Mountains and visit some of the local towns. When I reported this to the FBI, they said, "Well, sure, he is a KGB agent, and he has responsibility for all the émigrés from Eastern Europe, and this is the annual celebration out in West Virginia."

They were appreciative.

I did this kind of spy-work for a while. I cannot say whether my contributions were of any real use to the FBI. I'm sure that I have a file with the FBI, and I imagine that it's a rather positive one. Now, whether that qualifies me as a spy or former spy, I don't know. But it was an unusual and entertaining experience, nonetheless.

Kenya

At the same time that I was helping out the FBI and practicing at the IRS, I was getting involved in a diplomatic program in Washington, DC, called THIS, The Hospitality and Information Service, a program set up by the wife of John Foster Dulles, the secretary of state under Dwight Eisenhower and a former New York senator. I was with the Young Adults Committee, which provided an introduction for young diplomats to Washington, DC by taking them around to the different institutions and agencies and introducing them to different people in the Washington community. My wife was the vice-chairwoman of the committee, and we met so many interesting people, the most interesting of whom turned out to be the husband of the chairwoman, Dr. Johnstone Muthiora. Johnstone had come from Kenya to the United States eight years earlier to study and was then working on his PhD in political science. A fascinating character, he was teaching Swahili at the Foreign Service Institute, broadcasting in Swahili for the Voice of America, teaching African politics at the University of Virginia, *and* getting his PhD. As a point of history, when Jomo Kenyatta, the founder of Kenyan independence, understood that Kenya would gain independence from the British, he sent a thousand students to the United States to get university degrees so that the country would have citizens with university educations in English and Kenyatta could people the army, the universities, the government, and the business community on their return. It was a brilliant idea. Unfortunately, Johnstone didn't get one of these one thousand opportunities. Instead, however, his community in Dagoretti Corner, Nairobi held an auction with farm stock and produce, raised $4,000, and sent him to this little Catholic school in Washington State where he got his first exposure to the West. I met him after he had gone through his undergraduate and master's programs and was getting his PhD in political science, and we clicked at once. Johnstone didn't want to teach, and he didn't want to go into government. He wanted to be an entrepreneur and create his own business. I thought, "Well, that sounds pretty interesting. Let's talk about it." We did, and the more we talked over a period of months, the more interested I became in post-independence Kenya. I began wondering if I could raise some money and develop a business venture with Johnstone in Kenya.

In fact, I went ahead and raised $50,000 from contributions from nine friends, in addition to my own financial stake, and Johnstone and I became focused on setting up a little company in Nairobi. We weren't sure what we were going to do at that point, but I sensed that I might experiment with my life a little bit, move to Kenya, and see if I could create a role for an African entrepreneur.

The Kenyan government at that time was trying to develop a small business class of African entrepreneurs as they were taking over from the non-citizen Indian community which had long dominated the retail and wholesale business world in Kenya. I thought about it and talked to my wife who was a pretty adventuresome person herself, and, though she was pregnant at the time, she was equally taken with the prospect of moving to Kenya and pursuing a life there. To be honest, there are a couple of other factors. At that time, we had a somewhat uncomfortable relationship with my mother and stepfather. The tension between my wife and my mother was such that moving out of Washington for a while seemed a sensible decision. Fortunately, I could afford to experiment and, actually, after my father's death, I felt a freedom to take such a risk in a new environment that I would been unlikely to take had he been alive. And so it was decided: I would move to Nairobi with my wife and soon-to-be-born baby and explore these business opportunities. But first I would have to leave my job at the IRS.

From the IRS's point of view, they were quite unhappy that I was departing, especially considering that with a four-year commitment it was in the first two years that you learned and the second two that you contributed. If I had said to them that I was quitting this job to go off and work on Wall Street or a private law firm, where most of my then-colleagues went after their experience in the Chief Counsel's Office, I would have had a black mark with the IRS for the entirety of my career. But because I was heading off to do something so out of the ordinary as to set up a small business in Nairobi, Kenya, the IRS said, "Okay, you can be released from your commitment." Perhaps they said so because they thought that this person who they had hired was not entirely of sound mind. Who in this position would ever run off to Kenya to make a go at a new business venture? But then as I said goodbye to all my friends and colleagues, people who were about my age and likely to be recruited by major law firms, I braced myself for them to tell me how I was totally nuts. How could I give up this great opportunity to go into the senior levels of the tax practice and to do it at such a young age after getting the kind of experience we had all just had at the Chief Counsel's Office? But, in fact, when I talked to my peers, I received the opposite reaction. Almost every one of them said, to me, "Gee, that really sounds exciting. I wish I could do something like it. But I could never. I've gotten married, I have kids, school debts. I can't take that kind of risk." And that was the consistent reaction among my colleagues. They were amazed at my decision. And then, as I said my goodbyes to more senior people at the IRS, people who had stayed with the IRS and were building their government career, from them I got the same reaction: "I like what I do. But my god, if I'd had the opportunity to do something like travel the world back when I was your age—I would have, or at least I *should* have. Now I can't do it because I'm locked into this life."

For me to receive this kind of reaction from just about everyone at the Chief Counsel's Office of the IRS was greatly surprising but also motivating. It lifted me up and reassured me that despite the unusual nature of my decision, it could very well be the right one. One consequence of my move I really hadn't realized. At that time, I had a healthy relationship with both my sisters, Joan, younger than me by thirteen months and Nancy, younger by nine years. My years outside the US, not just in Kenya, but also my later years in London, distanced me from my sisters for most of my years abroad. I didn't do enough to keep these relationships strong. My sister, Joan, went through a series of three marriages and had her share of difficulties but did many things in her lifetime from becoming a CPA after her first marriage and later a provider of nutritional advice and life-coaching advice, and she remained the ever-optimistic woman through all of life's endeavors. My sister, Nancy, trained as a psychiatric social worker, had her own client base, but I relate to her best as an amateur political scientist, liberal, of course, and always ready to carry on a dialogue on world affairs. Both sisters had children whom Dominique (my wife of forty-five years) and I both enjoy, though we remain thousands of miles apart.

I moved to Nairobi in October 1969. Upon arriving there, I felt like a stranger in a new land. We didn't have a place to stay, but we managed to get a short-term lease above an Indian shop that had the fragrance of curry, something with which I was not familiar. It was just a little flat in the middle of the city, and it gave me the start to my life in Nairobi. After a few weeks, I found a house in a good part of town, and Johnstone and I embarked on a plan for our business venture. I had brought into my small team of shareholders a very prominent Washington architect who had some ideas about homebuilding, and Johnstone, myself, and this architect, Edmund Dreyfuss, discussed a project that would make sense for the immediate need that had arisen in Nairobi for middle-class housing mostly catering to the foreign community. We had already had some plans drawn up before leaving Washington, and early in my Nairobi days, I was introduced to a local architect, an Indian of Sikh extraction with a lot of Nairobi residential building experience. Together we assembled a vision for a property development and looked at the opportunities to buy plots that had already had residential, multi-family zoning and set about to develop our little project.

Now, at that time in Kenya, life was becoming more and more difficult for the Indian community. For one thing, the Kenyan government was beginning to encourage their citizens from so many disparate tribes to take on new commercial enterprises, in large part to compete with the Indian shopkeepers. On independence, the Kenyan government had allowed Indians—that is, those deriving from pre-independence India (Hindu, Muslim, or other)—to choose which citizenship they would like to have: Indian, Kenyan, or British. You could only choose one, though. The Indian community was rather clever, and if there were three brothers, they might select one citizenship each. But the point of my story here is that if an Indian didn't choose Kenyan citizenship, in order to stay in the country he needed a work permit. If he couldn't get a work permit because the Kenyan government was not giving permits to very many Indians, he had to have independent income (approximately £20,000 a year) and was then given an investor visa that allowed him to stay in the country along with his family. Therefore, a market existed for finding ways for Indian businessmen who had built retail or wholesale businesses to have some investment income, which would relieve the fear of being expelled from the country. This aspect of life in post-independence Kenya was an education in racial politics that I really had to learn from scratch. Likewise, about my new business partner: Johnstone had had a wonderfully diverse exposure while in the US, marrying into a vintage American Protestant family and mixing with students from all over the world. When he returned to Kenya, however, he resurrected his life with his Kikuyu friends from his earlier life. Evidence of this could be seen in our business plan:

Our plan was to build four middle-class town-houses, rent them out, and then sell them to an Indian investor. Indian businessmen were especially willing to buy this kind of property as long as when they did, they could use it to prove to the government that they had enough income to remain in the country (without the need for a work permit). My partner, a very loyal member of the Nairobi Kikuyu community, insisted on hiring only Kikuyu laborers, a Kikuyu foreman, and a Kikuyu contractor and purchasing supplies only from Kikuyu suppliers (including stones from Jomo Kenyatta's own quarry). We set up our own Kenyan company with our investors' funds called Haraka Housing Enterprise Ltd. ("Haraka" being the Swahili word for speedy.) Our entire investment was being built on a bank overdraft guaranteed by the only solvent director: me. Our two other Kenyan directors were the personal bodyguard for Jomo Kenyatta and the former Kikuyu judge in the Mau Mau Rebellion, now a retired schoolteacher. We never had a board meeting. The financial burden and pressures that came along with it were mine to carry alone. It took us a year to build those four townhouses, and we did it at half the quality and double the estimated cost. Nevertheless, we finished them, and they came out pretty well. I'll take credit for the tiling of the four townhouses, as for some unknown reason, the tiling people failed to show up to lay the tiles; and with the property due to be delivered the following week, my partner and I laid *all* the tiles in the four townhouses. This was quite an experience for me, a person who had never laid a tile, let alone cut a piece of wood in his life. But we managed to do it all and deliver the property on time. Interestingly, when it came to delivering the properties, we also had to guarantee the tenancies, because the purchaser would not buy unless he knew he had rent guaranteed for a year or two. This became very problematic for us. We rented out two of the units without a problem, but we could not rent the other two. Therefore, I personally had to go into the furniture-rental business and outfit two houses with furniture to allow someone to move into a furnished place. So, not only was I in the property development business, I was also all of a sudden in the interior design business.

We sold the properties at a good price, and it was enough for us to do two things with the proceeds: most important, pay off the bank so that I could be off the hook for the debt. But we also bought some land, which we eventually sold at a good profit. The balance of the money went into a factory. Now, my partner was pretty well connected politically, and the government was offering opportunities to local entrepreneurs, little types of projects in what was called the Nairobi Industrial Estates. We made an application for a grant, and lo and behold, we were given the exclusive monopoly on the manufacturing and distribution of shoe eyelets. Now, you might say, "What is a shoe eyelet?" But most people at some point today will very likely lay eyes on one. They are the little metal holes that you put your shoelaces through. Being granted an exclusive monopoly on shoe eyelets meant that no one else could import shoe eyelets and no one could compete with us in manufacturing their own shoe eyelets. We had sheet metal, which we imported from Germany, and we had the stamping presses for the shoe eyelets from India.

If you're imagining that my entrepreneurial quest ended with home development, furniture rental, and the manufacturing of shoe eyelets, you would be mistaken. No, at the same time, Johnstone and I found an opportunity to buy some mineral rights out in a very dry part of the country where there was allegedly gold and copper. We knew we needed to have an engineer inspect the site to see if there really was anything of value in the ground. I actually had a small investment in an Australian oil company, and I wrote the president of that company, James Buckley (the brother of the well-known US political commentator and author, William Buckley) about the potential opportunity for mineral rights. Sure enough, I heard back from him, and he said that it so happened their chief engineer was on his way from South Africa back to America and was willing to stop over in Kenya and see what if anything we had. So, we sent him out with a guide to the area that had the rights we allegedly controlled. And he went out to the "bush" and was really very helpful. What he found was neither gold nor copper, but a deposit of beryllium, a marketable commodity. We took a look at it and had to make a decision as to whether we would take this venture any further. However, the beryllium deposit wasn't substantial enough to invest any further, so we passed on it. But it was very interesting because I got acquainted with the Australian mining company and was able to glean what it was like to do this sort of exploration.

Meanwhile, when we finally finished the town-houses, sold them, and were preparing to start the shoe eyelet factory, I found myself not especially busy and was considering how to expand my opportunities. I didn't have great contacts in Kenya, especially because I was known as the American who had been with the Internal Revenue Service. Essentially this made me persona non grata with the entire American community, because they assumed that I was really a special agent of the Internal Revenue Service investigating entrepreneurial Americans floating in and out of Kenya that were doing things that were probably not reported to the IRS. So the first half of my time in Kenya, we didn't have any American friends, and I couldn't turn to Americans for any opportunities at all.

Nevertheless, I did meet the people who were running the East and Central Africa Division of USAID, the United States Agency for International Development, who had been asked to help with a study being put together by UNDP, the United Nations Development Programme. A Canadian economist had assembled a unit of people who would work for the industrial studies unit of the East African Development Bank. The bank was funded by the three East African governments of the then–East African Community, Uganda, Kenya, and Tanzania, and three of the major British banks raised a lot of money for industrial investment in the region. The industrial studies unit of the bank needed a lawyer to work on a project designed to encourage foreign companies to invest in the East African Community. I talked to the people at USAID, and they said that I would be a perfect fit for this role—and I said why not?

They hired me to be the lawyer for the group. The bank was located in the capital of Uganda, Kampala, and I would go there from time to time. My job was to analyze the legal environment of foreign investment in East Africa and to write a report on what the laws were and how they were enforced. I spent six months traveling around Kenya, Uganda, and Tanzania interviewing everyone, accountants, lawyers, ministers, people whose properties had been nationalized, people in government, and so forth, and it was absolutely fascinating for me. One day, I visited the British American Tobacco headquarters in Dar es Salaam, on the Tanzania coast, which was headed up by a delightful British gentleman who was still in charge even after the property had been nationalized by Julius Nyerere, the leader of Tanzania. Nyerere was a teacher and very much an ideological socialist in the sense that much of the land, especially in the tribal areas of Tanzania, didn't have the concept of private owner-ship. They believed in collective ownership. I was introduced to some people whose properties had been nationalized. The British gentleman from BAT took me onto his back porch, and he showed me the expansive land there and he said, "Well, the Tanzania government nationalized us. They didn't pay for the land, but they gave us fifteen shillings per coconut tree. Therefore, we were paid some money and I still have my position running this company." The result was a report for the bank and the only law review article I would ever write, this one on the legal environment for foreign investment in East Africa published in the June 1972 issue of the *East African Law Journal.*

Before the paper was ever published, I was asked to teach a course at University College Nairobi on foreign investment in East Africa. I lectured twenty-five somewhat radical students in the graduate history program on why they should believe in foreign investment coming into their countries. We had quite a spirited class, and we ended with a sincere respect for each of our perspectives. Kenyan students tended to be the strongest believers in a free enterprise system. Tanzania students tended to side with Julius Nyerere's vision of African socialism. Uganda students were the most split—observing the nationalization of the fifteen biggest Ugandan companies, all Indian owned, followed by the rampage of the rule of Idi Amin.

Margulies and Sterling

Despite all of these amazing experiences, by 1971, it had become clear to me that I was not really going to spend the rest of my life in Kenya trying to turn a small company into a big company. I had to leave Africa. I had to figure out what I was going to do with my life. Should I return to America and go back to the law? I couldn't say. I had some European contacts, mostly in the tax arena. There were lawyers in Rome, an accounting firm in Zurich who did a lot of work for Americans abroad, and a group that I had been referred to in Paris. I was more familiar with London than I was Rome, Zurich, or Paris, largely because I had a friend in London who I'd known since my time back attending Camp Robin Hood in New Hampshire as a camp counselor. He and I had even bought a little property in London which we rented out. So, yes, I knew someone in London.

After some conversation, my wife and I concluded that we were not ready to return to the United States and decided to spend a few years in Europe. But before we could commit to that path, I would have to see if I could land any work. After an incredible detour that she and I and our two-year-old daughter took through Iran where we traveled from Tehran to Persepolis, exploring the country on the eve of the celebration of the 2,500th anniversary of the Persian Empire, my wife flew back to the United States for her brother's wedding, and I was left alone to wander around Europe and see what opportunities might exist. I went to Rome and visited the firm I had corresponded with. I checked in with the accountants in Zurich, where there was the possibility of my helping on the tax side for Americans abroad. Then I went to Paris and had a run-in with a senior lawyer of Coudert Brothers, a very famous lawyer named Charlie Torem. He ran his office like a tyrant. I said that I had been referred to him by an old friend of his and that I was a trained lawyer, a graduate of Yale and Harvard Law School with a master's in taxation from Georgetown, and he told me, "I don't have time to piss, much less give you advice."

To which, I said, "Well, *okay*."

But then I met with another Paris law firm, and they referred me to a couple of entrepreneurial American lawyers who were setting up in London: Barry Sterling, a Californian corporate transactional lawyer, and Irwin Margulies, a former executive vice president of Warner Bros. and a well-known entertainment lawyer in California and New York. The people at the Paris law firm told me that I ought to talk to Margulies and Sterling because they were just setting up and needed a tax lawyer. So that was how I got hooked into that opportunity in London. Margulies and Sterling hired me, as I would later say, "off the street."

Before that happened, however, I did talk to other firms about possibly joining them. This was a somewhat difficult time for me. It was early April 1971. My wife and I moved to London. We rented a flat on a three-month basis. I didn't have a job as of yet. One evening, I went out with an old classmate from Yale to a Russian restaurant on Hollywood Road in South Kensington. Returning from a boozy dinner and seated on the backseat of a Bentley, I listened to the words of Paul Simon and Art Garfunkel piping up through the speakers of the radio, singing the song, "Bridge Over Troubled Water." And that was how I felt, nostalgic and contemplative, wondering which direction I would take.

However, not long after, I made the deal with Margulies and Sterling, and that turned out to be a lifechanging event. First of all, I could buy a house instead of rent—and so I did. This went some way in bringing about a more settled feeling in a city that was not yet so familiar to me. And then my professional life at Margulies and Sterling quickly went into full motion. The first case I had, which was in some ways prescient—meaning it would give me a sense of where I would end up in the entertainment world—was in representing Samuel Bronston. Bronston was a major film producer—*El Cid* and *55 Days at Peking* were but two of his major successes—but he had fallen on hard times and was on the verge of bankruptcy and desperate to get money. I was asked to represent Samuel Bronston in an effort to help him get funds. To do that, Bronston's chosen agent would have to be given power of attorney so that he could go to Switzerland and help secure financing. But the power of attorney would have to be notarized at the Swiss Embassy in London. This seemed like a simple enough matter. However, when I told Bronston as much, he let me know that he wouldn't think of going to the Swiss Embassy. He still lived in a suite at the Park Lane Hotel, in central London, on credit; he insisted that the Swiss consul come to him. To my relief, the Swiss consul agreed to Bronston's demands, and we did execute power of attorney at the Park Lane Hotel so that Bronston's agent could go off to Switzerland on his behalf.

This taught me my first lesson about what so many film producers were like, even if they were on the verge of bankruptcy. Sam was charming, egotistical, carried a belief in himself and his ability to overcome obstacles that was truly impressive, and, as I was to learn going forward, he, as well as many others in this world, came from often very poor and sometimes perilous backgrounds, took many risks but carved out their driven lives. This was an important lesson, to be sure, as I was about to dive deep into a world that insisted that I be prepared for such unique and talented people.

Working with Margulies and Sterling, I would very quickly learn a whole lot more. Because of their international client base, I was becoming versed in the tax issues associated with being a foreigner moving to the UK. Moreover, Margulies and Sterling was not just a boutique firm of two partners and their associates; they were linked with a very powerful corporate firm in California called Wyman, Bautzer, Rothman & Kuchel. Through two of their best clients, I had some of my most interesting experiences with Margulies and Sterling. First, MGM had decided to dispose of all its production facilities throughout Europe and Japan. Though Wyman Bautzer was overall counsel for the whole transaction, we, in London, were responsible for Holland, France, and Italy; and I, specifically, was responsible for dealing with Italy. This undertaking was my initiation into dealing with a major international transaction and, especially, local laws on the labor side; that is to say, what it was like to fire people in jurisdictions that often had employment for life etched into their lifestyle. As I was used to the freewheeling labor system in the US where it was easy to hire and fire employees, this process was entirely new to me. And *I* had to do it in Italy—have I mentioned that I do not speak Italian?—and that was not an easy task. Nonetheless, MGM sold all its foreign production companies for around $25 million, and they had to allocate $6 million for termination of employment contracts because many of the people who worked in the production facilities at MGM went back some twenty to thirty years. This was an education on its own.

The next significant Wyman Bautzer client that I would work with was Kirk Kerkorian. Kirk was a major financier, investor, businessman, philanthropist, and at that time a controlling shareholder of MGM. He looked to the London office, and me in particular, to help examine the possibility of establishing a casino somewhere in Europe. I had the privilege of flying on Kirk's private aircraft with several of his senior executives from MGM, who were exploring sites for a casino in the south of Spain. That led interestingly to Kirk Kerkorian asking me to personally join him in Monaco to talk about what his plans were for developing deals in Europe. Again, I was just a kid—or so I thought myself as much, anyhow—but for whatever reason, Kerkorian believed I might be helpful to him. Perhaps he would even try to lure me away from Margulies and Sterling? I suspected as much. I flew to Monaco to meet Kerkorian to talk about how I might be of service to him. On the first night, we walked into the Monte Carlo Casino. Kirk said he would spend a little time at a roulette wheel. He put $10,000 on red—and hit red. He took the $20,000, put it on black—and hit black. Then he took the $40,000 off the table and stopped betting. We walked out of the casino with his having earned $30,000 in five minutes. By all means, this taught me something about risk-taking: that is, you can take a risk, but you have to know when to walk away.

While my London life was beginning to take shape, I did try to keep my Kenyan company alive. There was a new problem, however: my partner, Johnstone, was running for parliament and was doing so against a former foreign minister who was not especially liked by his constituents. And, in a primary battle in a one-party state, my partner, who grew up in that small bit of Nairobi called Dagoretti Corner, with a very well-beloved butcher for a father, won the election. This was absolutely amazing, but my partner was worried about his life. This I knew from my return to see him in 1974 before the election when he was carrying a loaded pistol around for protection. Soon after his election, while on a state visit to India, he picked up septicemia on the plane, and they flew him straight back to Nairobi and he was put into Nairobi City Hospital where he died two days later. Ironically, his political opponent was a doctor and also the chief resident physician at Nairobi City Hospital.

But with my partner having passed, I went to the Kenyan government, which now seemed ready for me to cut ties with the country and end my entrepreneurial exploits there, and I said, "You win. You want our shoe eyelet factory? You can *have* our shoe eyelet factory. Just give us our investment back." And they said that they appreciated that I was ready to move on from this business venture in their country, but that our shoe eyelet factory was located in the Nairobi Industrial Estates, and that this was a place only for locals to do business, not foreigners, so that they could not give me anything directly but would have to distribute the assets of the factory to Johnstone's estate. However, the government also said that Johnstone's estate was hopelessly bankrupt, and so they would now have to distribute our assets to—and I'll never forget the term they used—"the miscellaneous African creditors," to whom Johnstone presumably owed money. And so we lost everything. But by that time, I was fully ensconced in my new life in London, and it was time to finally close the door on Kenya.

CHAPTER TWO
"Bond...James Bond"

My professional involvement with the James Bond franchise is indirect, somewhat unusual, but nonetheless quite interesting. I had met both of the original Bond producers, Harry Saltzman and Cubby Broccoli, through my employer, Irwin Margulies. I had done some personal and tax work for Jane Seymour (Solitaire in the first Roger Moore Bond film, *Live and Let Die*). But my real exposure to the Bond world was through Maurice Binder. Maurice had been a well-known graphic designer during the early part of his career with Macy's and had managed to get himself involved in the creation of the titles and trailers for the Bond films. He was the very person who in 1962 crafted the famous title of James Bond walking down the street, whirling and firing through a gun barrel, the blood dripping off the barrel, that iconic introductory piece at the start of every Bond film. Has there been a better known or more loved title sequence? That was Maurice, his skill, his sensibility.

I met Maurice through a personal friend, Howard Karshan, a well-respected television distributor. Maurice was a typical American client living in the UK on a temporary basis, who filed tax returns as a US citizen and had to deal with the UK system. The two systems were not the same and often had very conflicting rules about how one was taxed. Assisting US citizens living and often working in the UK was a common theme that developed in my practice during the period after I left Margulies and Sterling in 1974, as I was trained as a US tax lawyer but had been in London long enough to learn about the taxation of the foreign community, especially Americans. Maurice, a short, bald, heavyset yet cuddly man, was particularly interesting, not only because he drove a 1963 US-made Chevy around the streets of London with a righthand drive, but because he was doing some really innovative work at the time. He would go on to do the title sequences to sixteen Bond films over the course of his lifetime, from the original *Dr. No*, to *Goldfinger*, to *Live and Let Die*, all the way through *Licence to Kill*. He was very busy in the film world then and highly sought after. But by conducting business with tax exposure in a foreign country, Maurice needed my help.

The UK system was a confiscatory system under the Labour Party in the early 1970s. The tax rates were as high as 83 percent on earned income and even up to 98 percent on unearned income in excess of £20,000. That's one reason why so many British people who were entrepreneurial or had a somewhat international career were prepared to consider moving. I did quite a lot of work for UK citizens moving outside the country, as it were. On the other hand, the UK government wished to encourage the rebuilding of the country after the war, and bringing in international business was very important to them. As long ago as 1948, the government started a program which is often described as the taxation of non-domiciled persons, one whose roots are outside the UK but now lives in the country for business, pleasure, or investment. The system that was developed by the UK government was especially attractive to foreigners because if a person was not domiciled in the United Kingdom, he was not taxed on his income earned outside the country—that is, unless that money was brought back directly or indirectly into the country. If I could design a program so that an individual didn't have to bring any foreign income into the country, because, for instance, that person lived off loan proceeds from a local (foreign) bank or brokerage house, if that was all that was done to bring in capital, no UK taxes were paid. Now that type of system has worked well since its inception, and it meant a person like Maurice paid tax on the income earned in the UK but no tax on the foreign income, unless it was remitted to the UK. (This protective system for the non-domiciled person has been markedly changed over the years to restrict the benefits for non-domiciled persons, but still provides an attractive system for "non-doms," at least for the first fifteen years of a UK residency.) With Maurice, I had to deal with someone in a position of having come over to the

UK as a graphic designer, who worked in the UK as a graphic designer and was taxed in the country as such. And then I had to deal with issues having to do with whether a portion of his work was conducted outside the UK, or whether he was employed or self-employed. Much of the planning relating to the American community dealt with these kinds of issues. In that sense, Maurice was a very common sort of client for me. I managed to get him through his tax issues, and in the course of that work, he and I became good friends.

In her book, *Alyce in Mauriceland*, Alyce Faye Eichelberger Cleese (the third, blonde, American wife of Monty Python legend John Cleese) provides the very best description of Maurice I have ever come across. The book was made privately by the Bond producers, and only twenty copies were ever printed. Before I share that description from my own copy of the book, I will mention that I was responsible for introducing Alyce and Maurice. I had met Alyce soon after she moved to the UK from Texas through a mutual friend during a dinner one evening at the Carlton Tower Hotel. My wife and I immediately hit it off with her, and a friendship was hatched. The following month, on the evening of our son's birth, Alyce came to the hospital to see the new baby and support us.

"I walked down the clinic to see Domy [my wife] and the baby, and a man with a bald head rose up, nothing else was visible, rounding the corner." Of course, that bald man was Maurice, who had also come to the hospital to be with us. To have both

Alyce and Maurice there on the day of our son's birth meant a great deal then as it does now. That it led to a meaningful friendship between Alyce and Maurice makes it all the more special.

"Maurice Binder," writes Alyce, in *Alyce in Maurice-land*. "The very name almost defines the concept of a movie title sequence. His legacy lives on to this day and is overwhelmingly significant at a time when the modern trend in films has been to do away with opening title sequences almost completely. With the James Bond films, however, the title sequence has become so embedded in the framework of the franchise that it would be unthinkable for it not to be there, and the success of the title sequence can be attributed to just one man: Maurice Binder.

"Maurice's style was instantly identifiable. He had the ability to connect the titles to the script and the music or song, bringing them together in an incredibly powerful way. His crowning glory was the design of the gun-barrel scene, which begins most Bond movies. It is instantly recognizable, even if you have never seen a Bond film. For this image alone, Maurice deserves unswerving recognition. It is with this gun-barrel image that it all began, back in 1962."

As for that larger-than-life title sequence, Maurice never let me forget that he was deprived of a very big opportunity. The fact is, Maurice had been so happy to get the work on the 1962 original Bond film, *Dr. No*, that he never thought about negotiating anything that had a contingent element to it relating to future Bond films. His design work is what is called a "work for hire," that is, the copy-rights belonged to the production company, possibly even the original distributors, MGM, and Maurice was paid only a fee. He progressively received more money for his work on the Bond films, but in today's world, a very prominent designer may be in a position to negotiate even a small fraction of the income derived from the film. There would not have been any possibility of negotiating this in 1962. Mauice brought this up throughout our years of friendship. He wasn't furious. That wasn't his way. But he did want it to be known that he deserved much greater proceeds from that central piece of the Bond franchise.

Speaking of central pieces of the Bond franchise, I received a panicked phone call from Maurice on a Friday evening. He was on the set of the Bond film, *The Spy Who Loved Me*. He said that he had met a new Bond Girl, Barbara Bach, on the set who really needed my help. Bach had just finished a modeling stint in Italy and was a Bond Girl for the next film which would be released the following June. She had just been presented with a contract from *Playboy* magazine, as the magazine always wanted to photo-graph the latest Bond Girls, with the issue released in advance of the film's opening. Bach had received the contract and was scared to death, as the terms were such that her naked image could be used all over the world for one modest sum and with her maintaining no control over the pictures or the text. Maurice acknowledged that it was late on a Friday evening, but the photo shoot was on Sunday and he wanted to know if I could I help her. I talked to my devoted secretary, Moira D'Olivera, who at the time had been with me longer than either of my wives, and I asked her if she could stay late. Moira said that sure, she would stay late, just as well to protect me from this beautiful blonde bombshell who came into my office on St. James's Street soon after in tight dark jeans and boots, with flowing blonde hair. We worked until late that night, redid the entire contract for *Playboy*, and ultimately *Playboy* agreed that she could have veto power—power of cutting the text and all the photographs—that she would agree to only one set of photographs and text for the English-speaking magazine, and that everything else had to be renegotiated, including the use of the photographs in any other jurisdictions, any other languages, and so forth.

Sure enough, if you look at that issue of *Playboy* magazine with Barbara Bach, hers are the most discreet set of photographs I believe *Playboy* has ever published. Barbara was very appreciative of my work. She said to send her a bill, which I did, and she immediately sent me back a check. I had thought that Barbara, who would soon marry Ringo Starr, was Italian because she had come out of Italy on her modeling assignments. But I was very wrong. When I received her check, it had come from a Queens, New York bank and was signed by a Barbara Goldbach. She was the Jewish Bond Girl! I should have kept the check as a memento. It was certainly a revelation to me.

Maurice Binder, my beloved friend, passed away in 1991 of lung cancer. I happened to be on a trip to Egypt at the time with Alyce and her husband, John Cleese, and twenty or so of their friends.

"To be honest," writes Alyce in her book about our friend, "Maurice seemed to be doing fine. I thought there would probably be some time before he became very ill. I certainly didn't think he was at death's door. We returned home one morning quite early. I just walked in and flipped on the answering machine. Maurice's voice was the first one to play. He told me he was going to a faith healer in the country and would be there for a few days. He felt it would definitely make him feel better. This was so not Maurice and given that he was Jewish was also a long stretch from his own beliefs. The second message was from Sean Connery. In his deep Scottish voice: 'Alyce Faye, Maurice is dead. I am so sorry.' This was the first time I was made aware of his dying. Of course, after that, there were many messages and telephone calls.

"I was asked to speak at the memorial but upon our return from Egypt it was discovered that I needed emergency surgery and would only be allowed out of the hospital on the morning of the service. It was a wonderful service, Ian Johnstone, the film critic, gave the main tribute. Several of Maurice's close friends spoke."

Including me, yes. I gave my own memory of Maurice and told the story of his introducing me to Barbara Bach. Eon Productions, the producer of the Bond films, provided a marvelous film collage of all of Maurice's Bond film work as well as much of his other graphic design work. After the service, we went to the burial grounds, and Maurice was laid to rest. Having no children or wife, Maurice had never written a will. His assets passed to his brother's daughter, despite their having had very little or no relationship. The next step was to probate his estate. It was important that he remain non-domiciled in the United Kingdom to avoid exposure in the UK, with the inheritance taxes being what they were. We sought to get the probate of his estate into Florida. On what basis? Why, Maurice's clothes had been left hanging in a closet in his brother's apartment *in* Florida. Yes, that was all it took—and jurisdiction over Maurice's estate was done in the State of Florida. I was pleased to do this one last piece of work for him, a piece that brought him back, if only in legal terms, to his home country.

Maurice was a wonderful friend, whose legacy endures to this day.

* * *

But of all the people I've known related to the Bond films, John Barry provided the deepest relationship. John is one of the greatest film score arrangers, composers, orchestrators and conductors of all time. He won five Oscars for his compositions, including *The Lion in Winter*, *Midnight Cowboy*, *Born Free*, *Out of Africa*, and *Dances with Wolves*. But in the early 1960s, at the age of twenty-six, before he had won any of those awards, when he was but a young rock 'n' roller in the John Barry Seven with a pair of hits to his name, John received what would become the biggest opportunity of his life. A film was being made called *Dr. No* about a British Secret Intelligence Service agent called James Bond. The producers of the film, Cubby Broccoli and Harry Saltzman, were dissatisfied with the work of the film composer that they had hired on for the job, Monty Norman. John was brought in to rearrange the Bond theme. Perhaps if John had not been so new to the industry, if he hadn't been just so happy to get the work, *and* if he had been properly advised, he might have negotiated at least a joint copyright. But his agreement with Broccoli and Saltzman was done on a handshake. And so despite John's going on to do the arranging, composing, and often the orchestration and conducting, for ten more Bond films, and despite John's having reworked the original composition into its iconic arrangement, John Barry is not credited with any authorship on the Bond theme. Fact is, though a musical genius, John had no sense of business. In large part, that lack of attention to his financial life was what brought us together in the first place.

We met in 1978. It was through the actress Jane Seymour, who I had done some work for, that John and his wife, Laurie, were introduced to me. John had been dealing with a major tax issue with the Inland Revenue. In short, he owed the Inland Revenue roughly £134,000 and had gone to the US to work and earn money in Hollywood. Unfortunately, his departure, in light of his carrying such a substantial UK tax liability, created tension with the Inland Revenue. They believed that John had possibly fled from the UK to avoid his tax liability. His wife of thirty-three years, Laurie, describes his difficult position then:

> "John was an artist who was not interested in any of the financial aspects of his career. He let others handle any and all monetary issues in his life. He was naïve. He trusted people in business. He signed power-of-attorney over to business managers and accountants and lawyers and they could sign his name and set up bank accounts in his name and offshore accounts in his name—and they *did*. Meanwhile, John was a workaholic. In the '60s and '70s, he worked on up to five films a year sometimes, plus television. Then he woke up one day with a letter from the Inland Revenue saying: 'You didn't pay your taxes.' And John's reaction was, 'What do you mean *I* didn't pay? I have all these people who are supposed to take care of me and they didn't.' So he was stuck in a hard place where he had to pay his bills. He had to earn a living and pay for family. And where there was work for him was in the US. He didn't go to avoid paying

taxes. He *had* no money to pay taxes with. He had nothing. He was empty. But Chuck was the reason John ultimately got back home. No one could restore John to the UK until we met Charles Lubar. No one. Chuck is the savior and hero who got John Barry back to his beloved country of birth, where his family and friends and home and everyone were to be able to live and breathe and be in the UK again and to get him back to all the studios he loved."

The circumstances were dire. John was blocked from returning to the UK. In that period, some five years, he was not allowed to go to his father's nor mother's funeral. No, sadly, he couldn't go back to say goodbye to his parents because the Inland Revenue would have arrested him. It was said that an officer was even there at the cemetery during his father's burial and was prepared to arrest him. In John's case, this was not just a failure to pay taxes. The allegations were criminal tax evasion.

"Not being able to go back to the funeral of his father in 1980 was a terrible blow," says Laurie. "His mom died in 1981. We were in Paris for around four or five months and John was doing work on the Bond film *Moonraker* there. I flew to England. I used to go to visit her, flying from Paris. But John still couldn't get into the UK. His mother died and John couldn't even see her in the time leading up to her death."

I began to push the Inland Revenue and explained, "Listen, we really want to sort something out here. My client has a battle with the Inland Revenue going back some years and I want to straighten all of that out." I reached an agreement with the Inland Revenue in late 1982 that allowed John to come back to the UK, just in time for the filming of *Octopussy*. He was so ecstatic being able to return. His life in London had been so rich for so many years.

"John had the places that he wanted to visit, his routine," says Laurie. "Going to Harrod's food hall to buy his favorite things. He loved Wilton's Restaurant. He loved Rules Restaurant, the oldest restaurant in London. The streets of London were his home. Chelsea and Knightsbridge were where he lived his entire adult life, from a very young age."

I served as personal counsel to John Barry for the rest of his life. My wife, Dominique, and I were also good friends with John and Laurie. We socialized, we had meals together, we visited each other's homes often.

"John wasn't friends with his business managers or accountants or lawyers *ever*," says Laurie. "You were the only one, Chuck. You had *that* honor as well."

* * *

But we almost lost John well before his time. He had begun to regularly indulge in a health drink that looked like black ink and probably should have been mixed with water. John enjoyed the drink so much that he took a lot of it and ruptured his esophagus and almost died. "He was as good as dead," says Laurie. "Eleven weeks in ICU was not a fun place to be and he barely survived the multiple surgeries. The drink was actually made by monks and it was a concoction of herbs and all kinds of things—and he just drank it, thinking it was a health cure, and it actually poisoned him."

We looked very carefully at bringing a legal action against the company that made the health tonic. But the company that owned the drink never had the financial resources to make it worth our while. And John was just so grateful to be alive and healthy, and he just wanted to get back to work.

"But he was told that he wouldn't work again," says Laurie. "The head of pulmonology at New York Hospita told him: 'You've had both your lungs collapse. If you *do* work, you'll never be able to conduct. Just be prepared for that.' Well, that's not John Barry. And that's not me. I said, 'You can never come back in my husband's room again. That was a really bad thing to tell him.'"

During his recovery, Oliver Stone contacted John about scoring one of his films. But John wasn't ready, and Laurie told him that he shouldn't go back to work until he was 100 percent. So John waited, and he convalesced, and the first film he went to work on after returning to full strength was *Dances with Wolves*. Not only did he write all of the music, but he conducted every single note of it and also won the Academy Award for best score. That's the kind of person John was.

Meanwhile, in 1997, John and Laurie's neighbor and friend, Rupert Murdoch, was so incensed about John not receiving royalties for the original composition of the Bond theme throughout almost four decades of the song's tremendous success that he published an article in the *London Times* over which Monty Norman would end up suing the paper and winning a settlement in a defamation case. According to the court records, the article wrote that John had "waited 35 years to publish his claim. Associates say he was just 'picking his time to put the record straight'...In a sworn statement, Barry said, 'If I didn't do it, why did they [the Bond film producers] not continue to employ Mr. Norman for the following Bond movies.'"

In the court records, it says that:

> "the defamatory, natural and ordinary meanings attributed to the words complained of are to be found in para. 4 of the Statement of Claim:
>
> 'In their natural and ordinary meaning, the said words meant and were understood to mean that the likely truth is
>
> '4.1 that the James Bond theme was written not by the Plaintiff, as he has claimed for some 35 years, but by John Barry;
>
> '4.2 that the Plaintiff's claim to have written the theme was therefore false and dishonest;

> '4.3 that for some 35 years the Plaintiff, a little-known and unsuccessful musician, has been living a quiet life dishonestly gathering in the royalties for the hugely successful James Bond theme, to which he knew the Oscar-winning and highly successful John Barry was entitled.'"

Though of course the case would mean nothing as far as the public authorship of the Bond theme, it was a moment for John to speak honestly, and under oath, about his feelings for the song's controversial history concerning Norman. This was worth a lot to John.

"When John died," says Laurie, "Monty Norman pushed his publicity as *the* creator of the Bond theme. But he was always scared of John. John had strong but unprintable words for Monty Norman and said he would go straight to hell because he knew the truth. While John was still alive, he tried to speak to Cubby Broccoli and let him know that it really wasn't fair because *he* had written the theme. And it has come up in dialogue over the years with the Broccoli family members at a personal level because they *are* personal friends of our family's. It's very complicated."

In 2011, John died of a heart attack, and Laurie and I, along with the participation of the Broccoli family, put together a wonderful memorial concert at Royal Albert Hall. It was a very special event. The Royal Philharmonic Orchestra played for free—ninety-plus musicians—because of their love of John Barry.

So many legends performed John's music that night as well, including Sir George Martin. Shirley Bassey sang for John. They had been on the road together as young upstart musicians, touring England and Ireland. Michael Caine was scheduled to speak in person, but he ended up on a film set that night and spoke via satellite. Timothy Dalton, who filled Bond's shoes following Roger Moore's run of films, gave a tribute to John. A film montage of John's work was shown. The event was meaningfully financed by the Broccoli Foundation, as Barbara Broccoli is a very good friend of Laurie's; and not only was she devoted to John as a person, but they had a close friendship, a true relationship that went back so many years.

"Barbara Broccoli never left my side from the time my husband died until after the memorial concert was done," says Laurie. "She almost gave me a heart attack because she booked the Royal Albert Hall for his memorial very soon after he died to give me something to do to keep me sane."

A good thing she did, because the night was not only a beautiful tribute to John, but it raised in excess of £150,000. With those funds, Laurie and I negotiated a deal with the Royal College of Music to create a John Barry Fellowship for Music Composition for young film composers. The fellowship continues to this day.

"But you know if we never met Chuck, who would have taken the care and had the brain power to deal with the Inland Revenue in the UK *and* with this famous film composer, who was not allowed back into his own country for so many years? It was such a mess. But John didn't read his mail and didn't sign things correctly. He came up in a time when he was famous in London and could sign his name anywhere. He could walk into any place, he had a house account everywhere. After John died, when I went through thirty archival boxes from his family home in Yorkshire, I said to our son, Jonpatrick,, who is a very talented artist, 'Jonpatrick,, make a collage of these ten thousand parking tickets of your father's from the streets of London.' His father parked his car illegally everywhere in London. He didn't care. And I don't know if he ever paid the bills. I said to John before he died about the boxes which had been sent from his family home to our house in London, 'Why don't we start going through them? Let's do a box a year.' He said, 'You will divorce me.' I said, 'I haven't divorced you yet. I'm probably not going to now.' 'If you go through those boxes with me, you *will* divorce me. But when I die, you'll have nothing to do and you'll miss me so much and I won't be here for when you get angry at me.' And he was absolutely right. You have no idea, going through those boxes, how angry I got. But he was a genius, John, and he wrote a hundred and twenty-five film scores and a lot of great music. So, he compensated, though the executive skills were seriously lacking. Very much so. But when you fall in love the way I did, when you see someone like John and who he was, I didn't care. I'm a fixer. I like to fix things."

I suppose I do, too.

All those wonderful times my wife and I had with John and Laurie Barry, none of it would have happened if not for my having fixed John's problem with the Inland Revenue. Well, it was an honor to get John home as it was to call him a friend. And it must be noted that there is a funny parallel with John and Maurice Binder. Yes, there was a similarity to their relationship to the Bond franchise, wasn't there? Maurice was a well-known graphic designer. He was asked to do the titles for the Bond film, *Dr. No.* He never got a copyright on the design. He was a work-for-hire. And, as noted, twenty years later, he would complain to me that if this had been today and he had been a well-known graphic designer, he would have negotiated a small cut. He would say, "I didn't need a lot. But this is an iconic and unique title!"

So neither John nor Maurice had a copyright in his respective signature work, but ultimately it mattered little in two such distinguished careers.

CHAPTER THREE
East Germany, Here I Come

After my summer vacation in 1974, I went back to London and to the law firm of Margulies and Sterling. Barry Sterling, the corporate transactional lawyer, had recently decided to return to California and settle there, joining a major Fortune 500 company as their general counsel, leaving Irwin Margulies to run their boutique practice. Irwin was a dealmaking entertainment lawyer, and I really had no great desire to stay with him for the rest of my legal career. I concluded, therefore, that I had to make a choice: did I want to go back to the US and perhaps go to work for a firm there; did I want to join another firm in London; or, did I wish to strike out on my own and see if I could build a practice in London? By that time, I had developed very good relationships with a wide variety of people in the entertainment industry, particularly in the American community abroad. For that reason, I had grounds to feel confident that starting my own firm was a viable option. But honestly, I didn't know how long it would take to get a firm off the ground. A year? Two years? In this instance, stepping away from Margulies and Sterling meant both leaping off into the unknown *and* forfeiting a very secure paycheck. One does need an income to survive. So, naturally, I did feel some sense of urgency in securing an initial client following. Though I had no lead, I decided that I had to take the chance and see what would come of starting my own law practice and being in control of my own destiny.

I had two major, fortuitous events occur at about the same time, which brought some stability to my fledgling law practice. Firstly, I had been working as European counsel to Ernest W. Hahn Inc., a shopping center developer on the West Coast of the United States who between the 1950s and the 1980s would build forty-five shopping malls in eighteen states, mostly in California. They had hired two American entrepreneurs living in Europe, one of whom was a good friend of mine. I was given the corporate transactional work for the company, as the company was looking to see if it could develop a regional shopping center in one major European city or another. As a result of doing this work for Ernest W. Hahn Inc., I became friendly with their in-house general counsel, a first-class lawyer named Jim Barrett. Barrett had made substantial money when Ernest W. Hahn Inc. went public and had invested in Chateau Montelena, a highly regarded vineyard in the Napa Valley. He was someone I admired and

trusted. I went to Jim, told him that I was planning
to set up my own law firm, and asked him if he would
be able to help arrange some kind of retainer that
would carry me for a year. Jim was supportive and
so kind as to remind me of his own history when he
too had gone out on his own and received support
from various clients, thereby enabling him to set up
his own practice years before he went to Ernest W.
Hahn Inc. We worked out an arrangement: I would
have a year's retainer with Ernest W. Hahn Inc., and
I would continue to do precisely what I had already
been doing for the company. It was important to
have that first retainer, but also, to have secured
my first firm client commitment took me over an
important psychological hurdle. Now I had some
breathing room, if only just a little.

Secondly, in early 1975, not long after I set up
my own practice, and with my first retainer under my
belt, I met a beautiful and very stylish French woman
who became my second wife, Dominique Grierson.
Our introduction came through Jane Lehrer, the
wife of the real estate lawyer with whom I negotiated
my first office. Dominique had just separated from
her South African husband. She was an interior
designer working with a prominent designer, David
Hicks, the son-in-law of Lord Mountbatten. Our first
date was something of a disaster. I was writing and
editing for a group of international tax publications.
The editorial group had its monthly dinner at a local
Chinese restaurant, and I invited Dominique to join
us. Eating relaxedly on the floor, I dozed off after
the first course, leaving Dominique with a bunch of

tax accountants and tax lawyers, none of whom she knew. I did manage to wake up and carry on our conversation, but she was none too happy. Nonetheless, I must have done something right because she did agree to a second date. On that night, I serenaded Dominique with my guitar and my moderately reasonable voice, and that was a start of a long romance that has now lasted forty-seven years.

Back to my legal history.

Not long after securing my first retainer with Ernest W. Hahn Inc., Jim Barrett called me and said that he had a potential client for me: the head of construction of Ernest W. Hahn Inc., Michael Hummel. Jim explained that Michael Hummel descended from quite a famous family in Europe— his great-great-grandfather had been a major figure in nineteenth-century Classical music—and the current family was having some serious legal problems that needed resolving.

Now Michael—or Mike as he was called—was not the kind of figure one would generally associate with the world of Classical music. Again, *his* world was construction, and he could not have been better suited for that role. He was a big and powerful man, six foot five—a mountain of a person—tough, strong-willed, smart, and driven, as any head of construction should be. But then Mike was more than that. He had great warmth, he was a good listener, and he had a strong sense of lineage for his famous family. After all, his concern was for his great-great-grandfather Johann Nepomuk Hummel and the composer's relationship with Mozart, Beethoven, Mendelssohn, Chopin, Liszt, Goethe, and other personages of the time. It caught me off guard to hear this head of construction speak of his relative this way. My mind's eye required a kind of adjustment, a refocusing, as it were.

But Mike and I got on very well. We were roughly the same age and shared many of the same interests. It was easy for us to talk to one another. Moreover, he appreciated that, like many other clients I would come to have, I was an American in Europe that he could trust. Being from the US, understanding the culture there, and yet being part of the local scenery in Europe—this was a natural drawing point for future clients, as it was for Mike. Once I knew what the major problem was for his family, I worked out a retainer with Mike and the Hummel family for a year, a retainer almost identical to the one which I had with Jim Barrett and Ernest W. Hahn Inc. And there it was, almost out of thin air as it had seemed to me then—I had set up my own practice in London with a £1000 overdraft and two retainers that carried me for coverage for the first year of my practice. I could not have asked for a better start. It was a great stroke of luck, the kind which anyone starting out in business absolutely hopes and prays for. The firm was on stable ground without my having to use any of my own money. For that strong start to my practice, for the calm and confidence with which I was able to proceed, I remain to this day eternally grateful to both Jim Barrett and Mike Hummel.

The help Mike Hummel and his family needed related to the valuable legacy of his great-great-grandfather, Johann Nepomuk Hummel, as well as the work of Johann's son, Carl, a nineteenth-century

German landscape painter of some repute, neither of whom I had ever heard of. Mike's aunt, Maria, living in La Selva, in the hills outside of Florence, had taken some incredibly valuable artifacts related to the family, including a substantial manuscript collection, and gifted it to the Goethe Museum in Dusseldorf with a right to revoke the gift before she died. Mike explained that Maria was afflicted with a brain tumor and was *non compos mentis*. Being in such a condition, she was not able to consider whether or not her gift to the Goethe Museum should be taken back into the family's hands before her death or left to them in perpetuity. Certainly the opportunity to make such a choice was the kind of decision one would want. Just consider her great-grandfather, Johann Hummel's, manuscript collection; there were letters between Hummel and many of his friends of the period: Beethoven, Liszt, Mendelssohn, Goethe, Schiller. In addition, there were original musical compositions that had been written by Hummel with actual notations from his teacher, Mozart. An absolutely special collection of artifacts related to Hummel—but with Maria unable to communicate her wishes for the future of the collection, something extraordinary had to be done. And that *something* was now my responsibility. My first job for the Hummels would be to break the gift to the Goethe Museum. That was the primary reason Mike Hummel had come to me. But how to go about it? I assured Mike Hummel there was a way. I just needed a little time.

Of course, while I was looking into how one went about breaking a gift in a foreign country, my curiosity as to just who Mike's great-great-grandfather was significantly grew. Who was this Johann Nepomuk Hummel? What I soon learned was that Hummel was quite likely the greatest of the all-but-forgotten figures of the time, bridging the move from the Classical to the Romantic era. Consider this: Mozart was so impressed by the seven-year-old Hummel's virtuosic piano playing that he took the small child into his Vienna apartment to live. As per the arrangement, Hummel would assist Mozart, and Mozart would teach the young Hummel a thing or two about how to play the piano. The young Hummel remained a resident of Mozart's apartment, under Mozart's tutelage, for two whole years. It was in this time that Mozart wrote *Don Giovanni,* and quite likely with the child-aged Hummel fetching the busy composer another quill or ink jar. Well, can't you see it? The young Hummel doing anything his great master and teacher required so that Mozart could finish his historic opera! But Hummel was also there for the death of Mozart's father, Leopold, *and* the passing of Mozart's son, Johann Thomas, which no doubt placed the young Hummel front and center for some of the darkest days of Mozart's life. Imagine Hummel, just a child, taking in the sorrows of Mozart and his wife, Constanze, and the impressions this must have left on him. And then to have seen Mozart leap right back into his work. What a front row seat the young Hummel had to a critical period in the life of he who is thought to be the greatest composer of all time. Now who knows how long the young Hummel might have stayed with Mozart had Hummel's ambitious father, himself a talented violinist and orchestral director, not been so eager to begin touring the child-prodigy throughout Europe so as to both earn an income and make a name for Hummel.

Interestingly, in that day, someone of Hummel's talents could find himself before a great range of audiences. On one night, for instance, Hummel might have performed for kings and queens. Then, on the next evening, Hummel might have been in a seedy tavern playing to the locals who may or not have been there to enjoy the musical offerings of this boy wonder. But the Hummels didn't appear to be especially picky in this way—and they went everywhere throughout Europe and beyond, to points as far north as Edinburgh, Scotland, where the young Hummel's performances were so well received that the family was inclined to remain in the Scottish capital for many months. The Hummels seemed prepared to stay wherever they were most wanted and highly valued. This was their life now: traveling and performing, with their eye on the young Hummel's rise in the world of classical music.

Their next stop on the tour was London. Joseph Haydn, already a famous composer, was especially generous with the young Hummel, who was given the opportunity to premier a Haydn piano trio. Moreover, King George III and Queen Charlotte invited the child to perform for them on many occasions. At this point, Hummel, still so young, was considered a very exciting new talent throughout Europe, a prodigy on par with that other young boy who some twenty years earlier had been toted about the continent and beyond to play for the courts: yes, Mozart, himself. The record shows that Hummel was very happy with the touring life. After four years on the road, it was not fatigue that put a stop to his seemingly never-ending touring but the tumult of the French Revolution. War was everywhere throughout the region. In fact, the Hummels reckoned it was time to get home to safety. That was not such an easy thing, as it were. While aboard a ship traveling to Holland, enemy gunfire brought by the French killed a passenger standing near the young Hummel. Afterward, the Hummels had to take refuge in the Hague for eight weeks. With the French staging an attack there, the Hummels escaped and made the long and dangerous trek back to Germany, eventually settling in Vienna, where the young Hummel became a pupil of none other than the composer Antonio Salieri.

It was in that period that Hummel and Beethoven would become, if not quite friends, then great competitors. As for their competition with one another, it was later said that Hummel recognized that he wasn't quite as dedicated to becoming as great a composer as Beethoven, that Hummel recognized in Beethoven not only a slightly more capable, talented composer than he, but also one who was willing to make all of the necessary sacrifices to become...well...a Ludwig van Beethoven. But at this time, unmistakably so, Hummel and Beethoven were competing for the crown of greatest musician in all of Vienna, the musical capital of the world. Perhaps Hummel, if less interested in competing with Beethoven on a musical front, had opted to do him one better as far as their romantic interest. For it is said that Beethoven was then in love with the woman who would become Hummel's wife, the singer Elisabeth Röckel. Beethoven's passion for Elizabeth never entirely ceased, and while on his deathbed, he would give her a lock of his hair. How intriguing that Johann Nepomuk Hummel's life had been so intertwined with the lives of both Mozart and Beethoven. Already so intrigued by this man's life—and yet what more would I learn about him?

Haydn was a major figure in Hummel's ascent, and it was at that time that the "Father of the Symphony" secured a twenty-four-year-old Hummel a tryout for the position as the Württemberg Court's Kapellmeister (the court musician). These were very difficult positions to come by and highly sought after by the most capable musicians of the time. Kappellmeisters were afforded a level of comfort and favor among the powerful. You could also say that these were the most stable opportunities for a musician of the day with a good, steady income. Hummel being one of the most talented of the new generation of musicians, it is of no great surprise that King Friedrich I thought highly of Hummel's audition and the position was granted to him. More surprising, however, was that just one week after being given the post, King Friedrich died and his son, the heir, Wilhelm, shut down all theaters in

Stuttgart to pay homage to his late father. When the period of mourning was over, Hummel was to learn that his new king and benefactor was not particularly fond of music. Finding his talents unappreciated and encountering difficulty at every turn, Hummel resigned the post. Not prone to self-pity, and hardly one to sit around, Hummel applied for the recently vacated Kappellmeister position to the court of Weimar.

Now at that time, Weimar was the true intellectual center, not only of Germany, but quite arguably all of Europe. Goethe was a member of ruler Archduke Carl August's privy council. Friedrich Schiller, whose poetry would influence generations of writers and poets and playwrights to come, had called Weimar home for thirty years. That is to say, should Hummel be given the Kappellmeister post in Weimar, he would be coming into a far more supportive environment than the one from which he had just departed. In Weimar, the necessity of music and art and literature did not have to be proven. Among all ranks of Weimar society, art, and especially music, was akin to religion. Fortunately, the Kappellmesiter position was granted to Hummel, and his family happily relocated to the city in central Germany. It was not long before Hummel became great friends with Goethe. He would often perform at the poet's home.

Hummel also began to devote himself to defending musicians' copyrights. He worked tirelessly to put a system in place that ensured that composers were paid when their compositions were performed. No musician had ever taken on this issue prior. (To think that in 2021, Bob Dylan sold his music catalogue for more than $300 million. Hopefully Dylan paid some gratitude to Hummel.) Hummel also wrote what was considered the definitive text on learning and playing the piano, a work called *A Complete Theoretical and Practical Course of Instruction on the Art of Playing the Piano Forte*, a 121-page document that laid out all the fundamentals to the piano education. This text was a very big deal in its day and sold thousands of copies back when sales of such numbers were extremely rare. Hummel's introduction to the book reads:

To The King

Sire,

Music may now be considered as holding the most distinguished rank among the Fine Arts since it is everywhere admitted to form an essential branch of polite Education. Nor is it undeserving of this distinction for by its benign and powerful influence upon the taste and feelings it greatly assists and promotes both intellectual and moral cultivation.

Of all instruments upon which it may be practiced, the Piano-Forte has for some time become the most generally in use.

Many elementary works for this instrument have appeared in print, but with a very few exceptions they may be considered rather as epitomes in which generally speaking what had already been said is repeated in a condensed form, though in other words and with a different arrangement; without any particular attention being paid to improvement and progress, or to the extended compass and increased capabilities of the instrument so that even down to the present day, not a few points have remained doubtful and unsettled....

On and on the introduction goes, providing quite a view into the composer's mind. The instructions provided by the composer over the pages ahead are without question a fulfillment of his promise to the king. We see firsthand that Hummel's dedication to the piano is absolute and that he is writing this document to ensure a prodigious future for the instrument and music, itself. Again, Hummel's book sold tremendously well. His life, in general, seemed to be going right. A period of highly successful touring followed. Everywhere he went, he seemed to make the acquaintance of the latest virtuosos coming up in the field. Of particular interest is Chopin, with whom Hummel would become a close friend and influence. Whether in Berlin, Warsaw, London, or Paris, the interest in Hummel as a performer was immense. But among musicians and composers, it was even greater. At this point in his life, to Chopin and to

Lizst and their peers, Hummel was a superstar. He had made a whole life for himself as a musician and composer, and he had been close with all the major figures of the previous era. Who else alive could have answered such intimate questions about Mozart *and* Beethoven, Haydn, and Schubert, who Hummel also called a friend?

Having never heard the Hummel name, I felt as if Mike was letting me in on one of the great secrets of Classical music. And why didn't I know Hummel and his music? Why was Hummel's name no longer spoken of, despite the fact that his influence on classical music, in particular the Classical and Romantic periods, lived on? From what I could glean, it appeared that it was in the shift from the Classical to the Romantic period where Hummel's compositions fell out of favor, thereafter never returning to any level of real prominence. Students of piano do not study his compositions; philharmonics do not perform them except in the rarest of occasions. Recordings of his work do exist, but they are few in number. Having heard from Mike about the life of his famous ancestor, I bought myself a record of a piano concerto and sat down in my living room to have a listen. Very much in the style of Mozart, airy and sympathetic, my curiosity in this great forgotten figure of Classical music deepened.

Johann's son, Carl, was a renowned nineteenth-century German landscape painter. His paintings of the Italian and Tyrolean Alps remain very highly regarded. Though never reaching the popularity, nor importance, of the leading landscape painter of the nineteenth-century Romantic era, Caspar David Friedrich, Carl's work does live on in the collections of many museums, including the Metropolitan Museum of Art in New York City. Carl had two children, one of whom was named Wilhelm. Wilhelm was an industrialist, the founder of the International Paint Company in England, and *he* had two children, including a son named Wilhelm Jr., the father of Mike Hummel, and a daughter, Maria. Maria had made a home for herself in Florence, which unfortunately would lead her into trouble with the Nazis, who accused her of deserting her German motherland. But it was her brother, Wilhelm Jr., who suffered most in the early parts of his life. Wilhelm Jr. had severe difficulties with learning, all of which seemed to have been attributable to his poor eyesight. No one in his family bothered to establish whether or not the child could see. Instead, he was branded a kind of embarrassment to their name. And so, what does a famous, cultured German family do with a son that is an embarrassment to them in the 1920s? They send him to America, of course.

William (as he was now to be known) was shipped off across the Atlantic, with no job and no prospects. He finally found employment—and more importantly, he was fitted with glasses so that he could see and learn. But he struggled to establish himself in any way that would be thought of as worthy of his family. He worked for forty years for United Aircraft, the aircraft manufacturer founded in 1934 in Hartford, Connecticut (it exists to this day as Raytheon Technologies). Eventually, William retired with his wife to Southern California in conditions that were far from ideal. There was no reason for him to think that he would ever live a better life than the one he was living where even the basic necessities were barely being met. Cast out by his family in his younger years, one could say that William never recovered his footing nor found a path toward a more stable life. But then, yes, just as it seemed as if all was barely manageable for William Hummel, one day came a reason to believe that something better lay ahead.

The shift in William's story began in late 1974 with the unfortunate news, however, that his sister, Maria, had developed a brain tumor and that she was *non compos mentis*. Before she lost her legal competence, though, the family arranged for Maria to grant a general power of attorney to William so that he could help her if she lost competence. Well, she had done so. Maria was in no state to legally act on her own—more specifically, to make decisions on what to do with the major family lineage which had come down to her and had been gifted with a right to revoke to the Goethe Museum before death. Regaining this heritage would be a path toward providing William with some comfort in his final years. But could we break the gift and get back this trove of valuables?

I turned to a good friend of mine, Christoff Bellstedt, who was a talented tax lawyer in Dusseldorf, the city in which Johann's lineage resided inside the walls of the Goethe Museum. I did not speak a word of German and needed a German speaker to help me work through the issues and communicate with all relevant parties. Needless to say, whether speaking English, German, or any other language, the Goethe Museum was not thrilled to hear from us. They had all but assumed the gift was theirs in perpetuity. We had to inform them that in fact it was not, and that we were there to take it back. Now then, if you are thinking that the representatives of the museum replied that they understood and that they would pack up Johann Hummel's relics and leave them with the doorman, you would be mistaken. Heated exchanges followed, with no one willing to give an inch. I realized that we would have to be more aggressive in our approach.

We would have to let them know that we were serious and that we would not back down. What was decided was that we would proceed against the city of Dusseldorf and the Goethe Museum, saying that they had taken advantage of Maria Hummel, that we would revoke the gift under the power of attorney, and that they would have to return it. Still, however, the museum was not budging. They did not want to part with Hummel's lineage. Perhaps they felt that they had to protect it for posterity, that this was their duty as a museum, and that to simply put these treasures into the hands of a single person without the wherewithal to care for them was wrong-headed. This was the conclusion we drew. Though my clients were the rightful owners of these posses- sions—and the Goethe Museum could, of course, recognize this fact—as an institution dedicated to the protection of such antiquities, they would like to play a role in their preservation. This figured into our striking a compromise, and after going around in circles for a year, we were finally able to strike a deal: the Goethe Museum agreed that we could revoke the gift.

I think part of it was honor and part of it was the embarrassment of looking like they were taking advantage of a sick, elderly woman. But the deal was such that after the gift was revoked, we turned around to the city of Dusseldorf and said, "You want the gift? You can buy it from us, and then you can put it back in the Goethe Museum." So, without even moving a piece of Hummel's lineage from any of the exhibition spaces, we took back the collection and sold it to the city of Dusseldorf. An elegant solution, we all thought.

What was most rewarding about the decision was that we received enough money from the city of Dusseldorf to move the owner, that is, the person who inherited all of these Hummel-related materials, William Hummel, out of the rough conditions in which he had been residing into a small, attractive house in San Diego with a swimming pool so that he could live in moderate comfort for the rest of his life. Mike was greatly pleased, as was I. To think of his father having been banished by his family as a child, sent to America with his poor vision and to then struggle throughout all of his life, for his family's lineage to now have rescued him from hard conditions seemed justified and deserved.

But as far as the Hummel lineage, this was only the beginning, as Maria died soon after we settled with the Goethe Museum.

The next thing I had to contend with was a portfolio of securities that had been passed down a generation to Maria Hummel and which were currently in her bank, many presumably inherited from her father. The portfolio had hardly traded in the last fifty years, some assets going back to roughly the year 1900. There were bonds from the city of Moscow; bonds from the Tientsin-Pukow Railway; and other railroad, steamship, and utility companies that had gone bankrupt or been nationalized by the Russian communist or Chinese communist governments. In today's world, the bond certificates trade as antique works of art; some were wonderfully crafted. But, for me, it was fascinating to go through this stuff. There were some legitimate stocks in there, some Hoffmann-LaRoche and Nestlé shares, for instance, with actual value. But we had to work through all those securities, removing those shares with value now effectively under the control of her brother, William, who did inherit them properly.

The paintings of Carl Hummel, Johann's son, the German landscape artist, were the next order of business. There were 106 paintings in the Weimar Art Collection, all signed by Carl Hummel, with the exception of eight paintings which were painted by one of his contemporaries, Preller, also a landscape artist. How to get these paintings back? For one thing, the Weimar Art Collection stood on the other side of the Berlin Wall, behind the Iron Curtain. You couldn't just give them a ring and announce yourself, state your intentions, prove your inheritance, and expect much of a response. We had no confidence that we would ever see these paintings in person, let alone return them to the Hummel Family.

Then, one day, in 1978, there was a most unexpected turn in the narrative: William and Mike Hummel received invitations from the East German government; indeed, there were six invitations, two for William and his wife, two for Mike and his wife, but also two for me and *my* wife, Dominique, to travel to Weimar, to celebrate the two hundredth anniversary of the birth of Johann Nepomuk Hummel at an event hosted by the East German government and the Franz Liszt School of Music. I couldn't believe it. We were being given access, and in no small way. Though these invitations related in no way to the paintings in the Weimar Art Collection, we used the visit to meet with the heads of the Weimar Art Collection to confirm that William Hummel was the legitimate heir of their famous and beloved composer, Johann Hummel, *and* the legitimate heir of Carl Hummel. This was a good start, a kind of progress, a reason to hope.

Personally, I was very excited to go to East Germany and see it for myself. Weimar was the heart of Communist East Germany—and this world of East Germany was concealed behind a wall where the freedom to pass in and out hardly existed. Who could not be curious and perhaps even a bit afraid?

As much as I wanted to see what had become of the great city of Weimar, this principal center of culture throughout the centuries (the 1920s had been the city's last boom of art, literature, and film), I did acknowledge a bit of risk here. I wondered, for instance, that when the time came to return home to London, whether they would allow me to leave. They would, wouldn't they? It brought me some peace of mind to be traveling under government auspices. Ours was a state visit. A spectacle was being made of it for all to see as a demonstration of the good life being lived behind the Iron Curtain. But driving across East Germany and into Weimar, right away, despite being quite interesting from the vantage of a Westerner, you saw how the circumstances were not good at all. For one thing, in those days, East Germany was bankrupt; and for a government, insolvency is a difficult thing to conceal. There was almost nothing in any of the shops; grocery stores had almost no food on the shelves; walking past clothing stores, you saw empty windows and little hanging inside on the racks. Disconcerting, worrisome to say the least. You naturally wondered whether the people were doing all right and subsisting. But what could we do about it then? We were guests of the East German government, and we were there to honor Johann Nepomuk Hummel.

Many events were scheduled, including one at the burial plot of Hummel at the Franz Liszt Cemetery in Weimar. We went to a palace where Hummel's music was being performed. It was completely candlelit inside, with no electricity being used, and we saw a very fine performance. We were in the front row listening to the performance, however, and all of a sudden, my wife burst out laughing. I couldn't begin to understand what was funny about these circumstances. When I asked her why she was laughing, she insisted that she would have to tell me later. Meanwhile, she kept laughing. Fortunately, she regained her composure and eventually explained to me what was so hilarious about what appeared a most dry and solemn occasion: it turned out that the chorus performance that evening had done a beautiful piece in French. Now then, I don't speak French especially well, and I certainly wasn't able to translate the words of the chorus in that moment. On the other hand, Dominique, a daughter of France, was having an altogether different experience, hearing these words sung by the Weimar chorus. In one beautiful verse, the soloist in all likelihood was trying to sing, "*J'ai pris mon coeur*," which is, "I have taken my heart," but the German soloist kept saying, "*J'ai pris mon cul*," which is, "I have taken my ass." Again and again and again, the singer sang these words, and each time, Dominique had burst out in laughter in the candlelit room where no other person had dared to utter a sound. We were both laughing about this the rest of the night (and still, on occasion, even to this day).

Of course, there was some business to attend to on this trip. Yes, ninety-eight works of Carl Hummel had been at the forefront of my mind since arriving in Weimar, and I had arranged to visit the Weimar

Art Collection. In preparing for this appointment, I had come bearing the ability to prove that my client, William Hummel, was the rightful inheritor of this art collection. I went to my meeting, was introduced to the representatives there, and was given a tour of the entire inventory of the collection. It was an incredible amount of work, so many paintings. And Carl Hummel having been a landscape painter—well, his canvases were absolutely enormous. After all, he was painting scenes from the Alps, and going small would not have made much sense. For us, this mattered. Why sure, it mattered whether everything we were seeking could fit in a bread box or whether we would need several large trucks to come away with it; but before any of these important matters could be discussed, I was finding myself absorbed by the paintings themselves—not, as it were, the front sides of the paintings, but their backs, on which the history of the twentieth century could be seen: here, a Nazi insignia on top of which was another insignia of a hammer and sickle. These paintings had survived so much war and occupation, 106 paintings in total, and how many countless battles? It was astounding. But I had to gather myself. Again, there was business to attend to, and the matter was not proving so easy to navigate. Yes, it seemed that as kind as the representatives of the Weimar Art Collection were being toward us, the curators and the managers of the museum said that these paintings were German history and that there was zero chance that my clients could have any of these paintings. *Sorry*. Though they did acknowledge that the proper owner was my client, the paintings were *their* heritage and so *goodbye*.

I left without any paintings.

The Hummel Family had every reason to believe that the paintings of their ancestor Carl Hummel were to remain forever in the hands of the Weimar Art Collection. I certainly thought as much. We didn't have any further discussions about acquiring the paintings, whether there was something that could be done, some legal or governmental route. Private property laws between East and West were hardly recognized. And then the Weimar Art Collection had every reason to want to hold onto the works of one of their favorite sons, Carl Hummel. To lose the paintings would be a blow.

But then some twelve years later, in 1989, when the wall came down and East Germany became a free East Germany, soon to be reunited with West Germany, I gave Mike Hummel a call and proposed giving another crack at the paintings in the Weimar Art Collection. New laws had been passed so that a lot of private property that had been confiscated from its rightful owners were being returned. Why not see what we could do as far as Carl Hummel's paintings? Mike thought this was an excellent idea. I boarded a plane and returned to Weimar. It looked much the same as it had been during my last visit in 1978. However, the grocery stores and the pharmacies were better stocked, and you could sense that life here had a semblance of normality. As I checked into the same hotel that I had during my last stay, I was quite aware of the seismic shift happening in

Weimar and throughout East Germany. I returned to the Weimar Art Collection, and asked, "Do you remember me?" I saw the same people, and they *did* remember. They were very hospitable, and they acknowledged that with the de-Communization of East Germany, it was time to give back this artwork to the Hummel Family. The law was now on our side. I made a deal with the curator and the manager of the Weimar Art Collection in which we took back one hundred paintings. We agreed they could keep four of the Hummel works which they thought the best and most representative, and two of the Preller paintings. In a little ceremony, we presented these works to the Weimar Art Collection. Of the ninety-four Carl Hummel paintings that were returned to the Hummel Family, we sent half to Sotheby's in Munich, where they were auctioned and sold. The other half were sent back to California and to the home of Michael Hummel, where the paintings were hung up on his walls. Fortunately, Mike's home had plenty of wall space, as, again, these paintings were very big. No question, of all the walls in California, nowhere were the Alps better represented than on Mike's walls.

But while in Weimar, I had also taken back two Hummel houses that had been nationalized. In time, I sold them off as well. But there had also been more Hummel property to attend to down in Italy. During Maria Hummel's life, while still healthy, she had wanted to sell her home in Florence, and she had taken steps to do so, coming to an arrangement with a German family which was big in the shoe distribution business and hoped to use this new property as a Southern European distribution center. We were ready to sell the house to them, but there was one tricky problem: the property was held in what is called a Liechtenstein Anstalt, in French, *establishment*. An Anstalt is like a one-person company, a separate legal entity, and it can be structured in such a way that it functions as a kind of trust. However, for Liechtenstein purposes, this was a separate legal entity, and the Anstalt was the title holder of the property.

We sold Maria Hummel's interest in the Anstalt, which also meant that we didn't have to change the title. The property could stay where it was, the land transfer taxes being quite high. However, after a 10 percent down payment, the German family, concerned that the Communists were taking over Italy at the next election, renounced the deal and defaulted on the remaining payment owed to the Hummels. Naturally, we kept the down payment, but we had the right to sue under the contract for the balance of the purchase price. The German family refused to pay and said that we should take the down payment, that they were walking, and that there was nothing we could do about it because under Italian law, a Liechtenstein Anstalt was not a recognized legal entity, and therefore this was an invalid contract.

The contract that I had negotiated with them had provided for arbitration in Vaduz under the laws of Liechtenstein, so we brought the action there. Of course, for the German family to argue in a Liechtenstein arbitration that a Liechtenstein entity was not a recognized legal entity was a difficult argument to make, but they were prepared to do so. There were three arbitrators. We had chosen the ex-president of the Supreme Court of Vaduz, who was now retired. Then there was a Liechtenstein lawyer, independent of our own local counsel and a respected figure in the legal community, as our choice of arbitrators. To our great surprise, their choice of an arbitrator was a German lawyer sporting a dueling scar who we suspected was a former Nazi. Why they chose him, I still have no idea. And so, we arbitrated. I was physically in the courtroom when it was done. (Yes, it was a courtroom we used, but this was an arbitration.) And not surprisingly, we won the arbitration: they said yes, the Liechtenstein Anstalt was a proper legal entity and could hold property and enter into contracts. We had a judgment, and then we decided to take that judgment to Germany because, under a reciprocal enforcement of judgment act between the two countries, if you had a judgment in Liechtenstein, you could enforce it in Germany—and we went to Germany to bring an action to enforce it. Ultimately, we settled. We got something more than our down payment, but not the full amount. We didn't get everything, but neither did we want to litigate this for the next few years. And so we settled, and again that was a pot of money that was available for the Hummel family.

In the early 1980s, I helped the Hummel family set up a charitable foundation called the Hummel Classical Foundation (under California law) with the idea that we would take some of the things that were now in the family as a result of our work together, plus the artwork still held and some of the items that were not gifted to the Goethe Museum in Dusseldorf, like the original Hummel piano forte, Beethoven's walking stick, Beethoven's death mask, and a lock of Beethoven's hair (originally given by Beethoven to Hummel's wife) in order to celebrate the Johann Nepomuk Hummel name. It seemed like the most fitting end to all we had done together. In practical terms, our work had been about inheritance, money, basic matters having to with ownership. But for me, throughout it all, there had been a question as to whether we weren't doing something bigger than all of that: that is, resurrecting an all-but-forgotten yet important figure of Classical music.

It is fair to conclude that Hummel needed someone, namely us, to give him a sort of phoenix-rising-from-the-ashes moment. And who, if not for us, would take on that responsibility? After having had this Hummel experience, knowing what I knew about the composer, I certainly believed he deserved a larger place in history than the one he had been given. A Hummel Classical Foundation seemed like a wonderful idea. But who would run it? A foundation of any kind required a special individual, one dedicated to the cause. My first thought was to ask whether there wasn't a younger member of the family who would be up for the challenge, to tap someone who might feel as if he/she were preserving a personal heritage, the very story of a famous forebear might yield the best result. Perhaps Mike Hummel's children then. But Mike didn't have any children from his current marriage. As for a prior marriage from which Mike had several children, a very uncomfortable divorce had transpired, which meant he was estranged from his kids. In the end, the full responsibility of getting the Hummel Classical Foundation off the ground fell to Mike. Permit me to say it one last time: Mike was a boisterous man, the head of construction at a major mall developer who behaved like the head of construction at a major mall developer. He might have had all this cultural heritage, but he was not an easy person and not the kind to head up a Classical music foundation.

Nevertheless, for a while, Mike did just that, and the Hummel Classical Foundation did come into being. We had discovered some of Hummel's work in the British Library and considered whether some of the interesting, lesser-known Hummel pieces shouldn't be performed in concert. In particular, there was a *Missa Solemnis*, Latin for solemn mass, a body of music that is traditional and often played during Easter and Christmas. We interested a very fine pianist at the Music School at the University of Iowa. She was a true Hummel enthusiast, well-versed in the composer's music. We also contacted the head of the Choral Society at Rutgers University, who were interested in Hummel's work, especially the choral compositions. Our intention was to do a concert of this *Missa Solemnis* in the Newark Cathedral. This was the first time the *Missa*

Solemnis had ever been performed in the United States, and it was the first time it had been played in almost two hundred years. But we did it, and the *New York Times* had its music critic write a review. Although the critic did not feel inclined to praise the night's performance, it is interesting to read from Edward Rothstein's May 3, 1982 review that "the concert heard Saturday night in the Sacred Heart Cathedral in Newark is not likely to start a renaissance of Hummel's sacred music. The *Missa Solemnis* in C was last heard in 1806; after this first modern performance under the direction of John Eric Floreen, such neglect did not seem a grievous injustice."

A harsh conclusion to put into print in the *New York Times*—after all, this was an important night for Johann Hummel and his legacy, and a great review might have created even more interest in Hummel and given the foundation some momentum to work with. Instead, it was not clear what the next move would be. The foundation was teetering under Mike's leadership, as I had feared it would, and in a short time it was discontinued. Eventually, Mike Hummel developed premature dementia. Unable to work, he was taken into hospital and finally passed away on June 6, 2012.

Mike had brought me on an incredible journey and was in large part responsible for getting my firm off the ground. As for the legacy of Johann Nepomuk Hummel, one never knows. History is fickle. The day might come when interest in his work, *his story*, finds a new audience, a new caretaker. Certainly, in his time, Hummel made his mark on Classical music. But perhaps most importantly, he had been there—*there* for Mozart, *there* for Beethoven, *there* for Haydn, for Chopin, for Liszt. He was right there, in quite arguably the greatest corridor of time in the history of music. For me, to have been brought into that world was one of the finest rewards of my professional life, an astounding piece to my own journey that could have never come about without having taken the risk of staying in London and starting my own firm. To be sure, since then, I have been one of the world's greatest fans of Johann Nepomuk Hummel.

CHAPTER FOUR

Miss Piggy Comes On to Kris Kristofferson and Other Muppet Tales

We all know Jim Henson as the revolutionary creator of the Muppets. But one thing that very few people are aware of is the smart business decision Henson made toward the beginning of his career, one that would affect the entire future of the Muppets and the Jim Henson Company. Henson was in the process of taking a group of his puppet characters—indeed, the Muppets, who he and his wife Jane, herself a puppeteer, had begun developing in 1958—and introducing them into a television program called *Sesame Street*. The year was 1969. There was no reason for Henson or anyone else to think of just what a juggernaut these Muppet characters would become in the time ahead. No one could have imagined Kermit the Frog nor Rowlf the Dog becoming major sensations. Although perhaps not *no one*. For Henson did something that suggested that he very well might have believed that his characters had real value worth protecting. While Henson gave *Sesame Street* the rights to use his characters and even waived any personal fees—performances fees, in particular—he insisted that he maintain ownership over the Muppet characters. In practice, this meant that Kermit the Frog could appear on Sesame Street and sing, dance, and pontificate, as he was wont to do. However, should Kermit ever wish to do any of the above, or much more, on any other program or in any capacity at all in the future, Kermit—that is, Jim Henson—would be within his legal rights to do so.

And that, of course, turned out to be a brilliant move, for Kermit and Rowlf and so many of the other Muppet characters who appeared originally on *Sesame Street* and became hugely popular on that program remained with Jim Henson as he developed his concept for a new televised format. What Henson determined was that he would try to put the Muppets together on a show of their own. Again, he didn't have to ask *Sesame Street* if he could do so. These were Henson's characters, his intellectual property. To try to stir up even more buzz within the industry, however, and to give those would-be financers and television networks a sense of what *The Muppet Show* would look like, Henson did two specials. One was a Valentine's Day show and the other, oddly enough, had the very un-Muppet-like title of *Sex and Violence.* At that point, Henson believed that these two specials, which aired in 1974 and 1975, respectively, would launch his *Muppet Show.* But to the surprise and disappointment of Henson, these two specials failed to convince a single major studio in the United States to bite on a show featuring the Muppets. That's right, Jim Henson could not find the financing for a Muppet show in the United States—and you better believe that he had inquired with anyone and everyone. No one wanted a show starring Kermit or Rowlf (and keep in mind that Rowlf had spent the 1960s making appearances on *The Ed Sullivan Show* and showing up often on the very popular *Jimmy Dean Show* and was a well-known and beloved commodity.) But in a twist that seems right out of one of the great Muppet movies to come, these puppets didn't take no for an answer. In fact, what they did—what *Henson* did— was look abroad for someone who believed in the Muppets. And the first place he looked was the UK.

Sir Lew Grade was an entrepreneur and media impresario, a cigar-smoking hellraiser who shared a physical resemblance to Alfred Hitchcock. Born in Russia, raised in the rough-and-tumble conditions of London's East End, he spent the early part of his career as a talent agent. The ever-ambitious Grade saw that television was the future and leapt headfirst into the business, playing an instrumental role in the creation of a consortium known as the Incorporated Television Company. ITC's focus was on syndicating British television shows around the world. (It should be of no surprise that the global popularity that would ultimately come for the Muppets would be at the hands of someone who was already thinking of how to extend the reach of television to all corners of the planet.) One year later, ITC merged with Associated Television, another British company focusing on television syndication deals, and Grade's career took off. With shows like *The Adventures of Robin Hood* and *The Saint*, which were hits around the world, Grade came to be viewed as one of, if not *the*, biggest power player in British television. It was while at the helm of Associated Television that Grade became aware of Henson and the puppeteer's pursuit of a British backer for the Muppet Show.

"The Muppets appealed to him on every level," said Grade's niece, the talent agent Anita Land. "It was transatlantic, it was for families, it was funny, it had music, dance and big stars. Out of all his many programs, [*The Muppet Show*] sums up Uncle Lew's approach to TV best."

Grade believed in Henson's vision, this idea of puppets and real people having these great exchanges play out on the screen. He thought it was entertaining and smart, a show that could appeal to both adults and children. He made an offer to finance at least one season of *The Muppet Show*, which he would broadcast throughout the world. There were certain geographic demands, however: namely that the show be produced in the UK at Borehamwood Studio, as a significant amount of the infrastructure that would be used in its creation was located there. And so Henson and his full *Muppet*

Show crew packed up their things and came over the pond to set up shop.

At that time, the only relationship I had had with the Muppets was through a man named Al Gottesman. Gottesman was an entertainment lawyer in New York and a very close confidant of Henson's. He was Henson's lawyer and had a strong interest in the entertainment industry. In 1974, I was recommended to Gottesman by a mutual friend for a peanut-sized problem, an intellectual property issue that the Muppets and Henson were facing in the European Communities. Gottesman asked if I would attend to the matter for them. Though I was not an intellectual property lawyer per se, I understood the issue and I helped them resolve it—for which I believe I was paid the nominal sum of one hundred pounds. Al Gottesman was appreciative, and that, as they say, was *that*. I didn't expect to ever hear from Gottesman again. Nor did I even think twice about whether or not I would. Naturally, clients of a certain stature stir up a kind of curiosity about the future, and one wonders if there won't be additional opportunities to come. But this was *not* that kind of situation, for who would ever think that anything would become of this group of puppeteers?

But then a year later, as Sir Lew Grade and Jim Henson were about to go into business together, Al Gottesman called me up again. He filled me in on their circumstances: Henson had been unable to drum up interest in the US, and he and all his puppeteers and craftsmen and women were picking up their stakes and crossing the Atlantic to the UK to make *The Muppet Show* with the backing of none other than Sir Lew Grade. It seemed like a great opportunity for them. Knowing that I was trained as a tax lawyer, Gottesman was seeking help with some structuring because he had been told that the UK corporate and individual tax rates were very high. He wanted to figure out a way, should they be successful, to send the profit element back to the United States. And he wanted to ensure that the puppeteers themselves were not confiscatorily taxed on their earnings. This was especially complicated because the full Muppets crew was American and all the work was being done in London, including the actual shooting of the program. The first series pilot would take about a year, and so they needed a tax structure. Could I help them? I assured Gottesman that I could. Creating this structure was my first task.

I worked very hard—long days, long nights—with a now-very-well-known tax barrister, Peter Whiteman, QC, and we came up with a structure for the production of the entire run of *The Muppet Show* (with options, of course). And the structure was such that, although production was in the UK, and all the puppeteers had to pay taxes for their work on *The Muppet Show* in the UK, matters were arranged in such a way that effectively meant that we could deliver off the product back to Henson in the United States so that the ultimate benefit would be to his US company, Henson Associates, rather than the profit being left in the United Kingdom at a much higher corporate tax rate. From the corporate side, we figured out how to have a UK company set up *as* the production company but signing a deal with the owner of the rights to *The Muppet Show* and the Muppet characters with Henson Associates back in the US. This gave, effectively, an arm's-length profit to the production company in the UK but kept the residual value back in the United States. We also designed a program for the puppeteers, most of whom were brought over from the United States, as to how they were taxed in the UK. At that time, the UK rates were exceptionally high, but there were quite favorable techniques for what were called the foreign domiciled community, that is, foreign persons who lived and worked in the UK. Also at that time, there was not a heavily developed program to go after stars or entertainers with respect to their performance activities when they were in the UK. That was an American tax issue. Many tax treaties were changed in later years so that Inland Revenue, the UK equivalent to the IRS, could specifically target entertainers and sportsmen and prevent them from sheltering behind their own wholly owned companies. But back when we set up the original *Muppet Show* structuring, the UK was relatively relaxed about this. That allowed me to go in and negotiate on behalf of the puppeteers with Inland Revenue so that they were taxed on a very modest basis, even though they also had to pay taxes in the United States, but with a full credit for taxes paid in the UK. So, we set up a structure, that a) let the profits, if there ever were any, go back to the United States, and b) did not make it more expensive for the puppeteers to perform in the UK, notwithstanding the very high rates for individuals.

One could very well ask as to why go through all of this trouble. What was the likelihood that this Muppet show would be all that successful, so successful that there would even be any future profits to protect? Who among us could imagine this production doing much of anything? However, once again there was Jim Henson, that visionary, looking ahead, protecting his future, and believing that he really was onto something quite extraordinary and potentially valuable. I went up to his house in Hampstead for a handful of meetings. Henson, like so many of the people who he had around him, was a real gentleman. He was a very thoughtful, likeable person. I could tell that he had incredible creative impulses and that he was willing to take real risks associated with his work. I met his wife, Jane, and two of their children, Lisa and Brian, who I did get to know briefly. I certainly didn't think it was a bad idea of Henson's to put in this extra effort with the tax structuring of his show. After all, that is my line of work. But the extra effort on putting together this structuring in these incipient years would soon pay enormous dividends. Just five years later, with *The Muppet Show* having been incredibly successful, the program went into syndication in the United States and that deal fetched upward of $100 million. Most of that income was brought back to the United States without major exposure in the UK. But it was Henson's thoughtfulness and his willingness to "invest" in his tax lawyers that paid such handsome profits to his company.

Granted, I was paid for my work (and much more work having to do with Henson and Al Gottesman, which I will describe in due course). But my greatest reward for all that structuring, the one that I hold dear above all the others, involved an invitation to come down to Borehamwood Studio and see a taping of *The Muppet Show*. Indeed, one day I received a phone call from Gottesman. He had heard that I was doing some work for the performing artist and songwriter (and later a film star) Kris Kristofferson, who was on a European tour and would be performing in London at the Royal Albert Hall in the days ahead. (Something that I did quite a lot of then was representing foreign artists performing in the United Kingdom to help them deal with the taxes they would incur as a result of their UK performances.) Kristofferson would also be appearing on *The Muppet Show*, and Gottesman thought that perhaps I would like to see the live taping. I said that this sounded like a great idea and I would love to come down to the studios to see Kris Kristofferson perform on *The Muppet Show*.

I admit, after all the work we had done together, I was excited to finally see *The Muppet Show*—the full production—in person. And what a production it was, with so many technical aspects having to do with the puppets and their staging, the lights, the cameras, the full crew. Of course, one thing that the Muppets were especially famous for were their musical numbers. But walking onto the soundstage that day in August of 1978, little did I know that I was about to see one of the great musical numbers in the history of *The Muppet Show*: Kris Kristofferson's performance of "Help Me Make It Through the Night," which he would sing to Miss Piggy (who, as any Muppet afficionado knows, was voiced by Frank Oz) becoming a true Muppets musical hit. Having been there in person to witness Kristofferson serenade Miss Piggy, I could see why. It was hilarious! It was brilliant! It was Henson and Oz at their best.

Before the song began, Miss Piggy was poking her head through the trademark red Muppet curtain to make sure Kermit wasn't close at hand. She didn't want him to be jealous that she was about to do such a romantic number with the very handsome Kris Kristofferson. So she claimed. Of course, that was *exactly* what Miss Piggy wanted and she began at the next moment to pretend that Kristofferson was making a move on her. Then the curtain drew back, revealing the country music legend with his long blond hair neatly combed, black blazer, blue button-down shirt, charming grin, with Miss Piggy, in a violet dress, close to Kristofferson, and the red-headed Muppet known as Animal in back on drums, among others.

Kristofferson began singing, pulling a pink ribbon from Miss Piggy's blond hair, which was also very well-groomed for the occasion. Miss Piggy shook her head from side to side, the pink ribbon falling from her hair to the floor. To the crowd's absolute delight, Miss Piggy was *oohing* and *ahhing* all the while, her eyes locked on Kristofferson's, their bodies close. She was, as they say, putty in his hands. And with Kristofferson serenading her in his casual country twang, Miss Piggy eventually thew herself on the country star, her arms flying open wide.

Kristofferson was doing everything in his power to hold back his laughter. It was Miss Piggy's hair, which she—Frank Oz—was throwing about one way and another in such a wildly dramatic fashion that was causing Kristofferson to laugh so hard. But then he delivered the song's eponymous line: "Help me make it through the night."

And Miss Piggy screamed, "Kris-sy!" swinging her whole body around and belting out the next lyric herself. Now Kristofferson just lost it. He was laughing hysterically, as was I, as was everyone on the Muppets sound stage. You couldn't believe what you were watching—it was true Muppet magic. However, Kristofferson, the consummate professional, getting back into the song, into character, sang on, drawing Miss Piggy's hair from her face and shoulders. And Miss Piggy sang along with him, her shrill manner notwithstanding. Kristofferson's hands were holding Miss Piggy's face, as if he were about to lay one on her. And staring deeply into each other's eyes, in unison, they sang:

"We don't want to be alone. Help me make it through the night."

Miss Piggy then let loose on Kristofferson, kissing him everywhere. Being that Miss Piggy didn't even come up to Kristofferson's shoulder, she was mostly just getting his chest. So, Kristofferson kindly bent down and kissed her on her...*snout*. And Animal in the background was pounding out a stinger on the drums, the audience, myself including, wildly applauding. It was such a thrill. It might be hard to believe, but I still feel so fortunate to have been in that room that day, there to experience firsthand the magic and electricity that was Henson, Oz, and that talented group of showmen. What an extraordinary time. One of the top ten *Muppet Shows* of the entire five-year series—and I was there! Was *this* really appropriate for children?

* * *

I had done a whole lot of work for the Muppets, mostly in television. But then Henson and his cohorts set their eyes on new horizons: the Hollywood feature. *The Muppet Movie*, the very first film to star the Muppets, was a tremendous success. Released in 1979, it featured a who's-who of the silver screen, from Mel Brooks to Steve Martin, Elliott Gould to Bob Hope. Even the legendary iconoclast and visionary Orson Welles popped up in the production. Cameos aside, *The Muppet Movie* grossed $65.2 million and garnered two Oscar nominations, including Best Original Song, for that wonderful Kermit the Frog number, "Rainbow Connection." Roger Ebert and Gene Siskel, the preeminent film critics of the day, both praised the movie. And Henson, Gottesman, Grade, and anyone associated with the world of the Muppets had every reason to feel optimistic about what lay ahead.

Al Gottesman called me up one day around that time and said that the Henson Company would now be doing a second Muppet film. The first film had been such a smash, how could they not? This second film, called *The Great Muppet Caper*, would be directed by Jim Henson. (The first film had been directed by James Frawley.) And where the first film had told the Muppets' origin story, this follow up would be about the Muppets finding themselves embroiled in a London jewel heist. Hearing him speak about it, I could tell that Gottesman was feeling especially optimistic about the success of this next Muppet feature. Meanwhile, there was another film that Henson had been putting together at that time. Gottesman described this other project to me, but he didn't do so with as much gusto and surety. It was kind of an oddball film, a dark story, one that would allow for Henson to go down some of the more unusual roads that he had been dreaming up. Gottesman said this "other" film would cost $25 million, and that he was discouraging Henson from even making it. But it was Henson's company, and he could do what he wanted. Between the two films, *The Great Muppet Caper* was definitely the safer bet. That's what Gottesman said. He wanted to know whether I could structure everything for them. I said that I most certainly could.

But how to go about doing this task? At the forefront of my mind, I had this notion that the second Muppet movie, *The Great Muppet Caper*, was a kind of guaranteed success, a shoe-in; and that this other film, which would be titled *The Dark Crystal*, would lose money for Henson Associates and ITC Entertainment, Sir Lew Grade's production company, who were also behind both films. Al Gottesman asked if there was any chance that we could do the production *offshore* and not take all the money back to the United States. I told him that this might be doable but that I would have to think about it. Ultimately, I did end up creating a structure for them that had been used by a number of Americans with active film businesses outside of the United States. In this instance, I set up a Netherlands-Antilles production company. That's right, Netherlands-Antilles. It is a small island in the Caribbean, about eleven hours flying from London. The structure was such that a Netherlands-Antilles production company would hire a UK production company to physically make the film, after which the UK production company would then deliver the film back to the Netherlands-Antilles production company. The system would be exploited in the United States, and a good portion of the active business royalty income for the creation and the distribution of the film would be through the Netherlands-Antilles. The structure we would put in place would keep a significant amount of money outside of the United States. Mind you, this was the 1970s, before some of the more complex rules came in that made it much more difficult to do this sort of thing—but it was a very exciting tax structure that we had put together. I even traveled with Gottesman to the Netherlands-Antilles for *actual* board meetings. Unfortunately, we did so in summer, which is hardly my idea of a holiday. It was some of the most intense heat I had ever encountered in my life. Gottesman and I both brought our tennis rackets, expecting to do a lot of playing while there. But we had to wake up at the crack of dawn or else wait for the sun to set in the evening to do so, the heat under that Caribbean sun too much to bear. Being a lawyer, I am not one to believe in signs. But perhaps this heat *was* a sign from above.

We had put together this complicated structure for *The Great Muppet Caper* and figured, "What the hell. It's the second Muppet movie. It's got to make a lot of money." And again, Gottesman reiterated over and over that *The Dark Crystal* was not the kind of happy-go-lucky, boisterous adventure story typical of the Muppets, the kind that appealed to everyone, children *and* adults. And for that reason, Gottesman explained that I shouldn't run my complicated tax structure through this second film because it wasn't going to make any money. We would therefore keep the film production in the United States for *The Dark Crystal* and take those losses against all the other income. I said fine, I agreed, this made a lot of sense.

So there I was, an international tax lawyer of some significance, giving Henson and Gottesman these structures. The only thing that I neglected to understand was the reality of the film business. I had seen a lot in the film industry by now—and I had seen some at the time I was putting together the structure. But I got this one completely wrong. The second Muppet film bombed, grossing $31.2 million, only half of what the first film had earned at the box office. Although Gene Siskel praised the Muppet follow-up, Roger Ebert was far less impressed, saying that the screenplay was not well-developed and describing the caper set-up as formulaic. But criticism or praise, I had all these losses outside of the United States, which I couldn't use. And then to make matters worse, lo and behold, *The Dark Crystal*, that flight of whimsey, that sure loser, was the sleeper film of 1982 and became a cult classic and an amazing success.

Oh. Dear.

So yes, I had all this profit back in the United States where I never intended it to be. It is a story I tell on myself because notwithstanding the brilliant thinking that went into whether to take the film production company offshore or to live with it in the United States, I got this one completely backward. I suppose I do not have to carry the burden of that failure alone, as I was joined by nearly all concerned parties in thinking that *The Great Muppet Caper* would be the second huge Muppet success and that *The Dark Crystal* would be their first sizeable loss. That is, with the exception of Jim Henson. It is highly unlikely that Henson viewed any of his work as sure to have either sizeable gains or losses. Henson was an optimist and an artist first, unconcerned with such things. And I remained happy with the work that I had done with the Muppets. Those experiences had been exciting and edifying. There were still more to come.

Sure enough, many years later, I was approached by Frank Oz, who I had gotten to know through the course of my time with the whole Muppet team. Again, Frank Oz was the puppeteer and voice behind Miss Piggy, as well as several other characters including Fozzie Bear, Animal, and Sam the Eagle. Jim Henson considered him one of the greatest puppeteers in the history of puppeteering. But his talents went well beyond the scope of such work. Oz would become a highly respected film director in the time to come.

Before any of that had begun to coalesce for him, however, Oz had been contacted by George Lucas. Lucas was making his Star Wars films, *The Empire Strikes Back* and then *Return of the Jedi,* and he had asked Oz to serve as the puppet and voice for none other than that *other* green icon, Yoda. At this time, Yoda was not yet on every child's lunchbox around the world, nor was he one of the most imitated film personae to ever grace the screen. Oz called me up and asked if I could help him sort out a very interesting matter concerning his role as Yoda. Consider this: to play the role of Yoda, Frank Oz would have to *perform* that gravelly, backward-talking voice, but he would also have a *technical role* as the puppeteer moving Yoda about and directing others in moving parts of Yoda's body. So then, what did this make Frank Oz as far as his role on the production of these two films? Was he a performer? A technician? This was particularly complicated because the rules by that time had recently changed, and Inland Revenue was coming down hard on performers. If an individual was serving in any other roles on a production—be that producer, director, writer, cinematographer, Inland Revenue did not bother. But with the support of progressive changes in the taxation of performing artists (and sportsmen), sanctioned by specific tax provisions in the tax treaties of most developed countries, performances in front of the camera were eminently attackable by Inland Revenue. Performance income could get very expensively taxed because Inland Revenue could look through corporations that may well have been set up for totally non-tax reasons, disregard the corporation, and tax performance income directly. We were potentially in for a battle with Inland Revenue. I worked with Frank Oz on the Yoda issue and did what I could for him. But all these years later, this question has not lost its fascination for me: is the person performing in the role of Yoda, for this example, a performer or a technician? These were the grounds on which I had to fight for Frank Oz and his legacy as the great artist behind that petite green Jedi Master known to just about everyone alive as Yoda. Having done so, I feel just a little bit closer to the Force.

Also, many years after my initial work for the Muppets, I would do more work for a whole group of Muppets that had come back over the pond to produce a film. I received a call from one of the puppeteers who I had worked with in the time when the Muppets were being produced in the UK and whose personal tax work I had done in the time since, named Dave Goltz. He was middle-aged by then and still a puppeteer. He said that he and about thirty colleagues needed my help with a structure.

In the interim, things had changed significantly (as indicated above), and it had become very difficult for performing artists to shelter much of their income that was attributable to their performances. I organized a very fine group of specialist accountants, who were doing a lot of entertainment negotiations with Inland Revenue. It was fun to reacquaint myself with this team of puppeteers. I could not help but think of how far they had all come in these last few decades, but also of how much had changed for them.

Of course, Henson had passed, having died tragically at fifty-three after contracting a strep infection that obliterated his lungs in just the blink of an eye and led to an insurmountable bout of pneumonia. His very bright and talented children, Brian and Lisa, were now driving the Henson Company forward into the future under the Disney Company umbrella. Frank Oz had moved on to direct many successful films, including the classic, *Dirty Rotten Scoundrels*. Sir Lew Grade had passed away. Al Gottesman was still practicing law, but he was no longer working with the Henson Company. I remain forever grateful for the time I spent with these visionaries. On occasion, I do like to cue up the video of Kris Kristofferson singing, "Help Me Make It Through the Night" to Miss Piggy. That song is part of my repertoire. I know it cold. I love to play it, for it brings me right back into Borehamwood Studios on that special day.

CHAPTER FIVE

The Linda Lovelace, Chuck Traynor, Marilyn Chambers Triumvirate

Linda Lovelace came into our office to see Irwin Margulies in the spring of 1974. The newly famous pornography star had become a sensation through the 1972 release of a film called *Deep Throat*, the first marriage of pornography (as defined) to mainstream film. At that time, Lovelace was married to Chuck Traynor, who has been described as a talent agent, pimp, and pornography star in his own right. Traynor claimed to have taken Lovelace out of a cheap pole-dancing house in Florida and turned her into an international star. But when Linda Lovelace appears in your office right off the heels of *Deep Throat*, there is most certainly a buzz throughout the halls. Everyone is curious to know why such a larger-than-life figure has come. And naturally, in the case of Lovelace, everyone wants to know what she looks like in the flesh. We had all seen her pictures in magazines, in newspapers, on television. But now she was in our presence: Linda Lovelace, the one and only. It seemed almost unreal. And yet there she was, siting across the table from Irwin Margulies, deep in discussion.

One day prior, Irwin had been contacted by the BBC and asked if he had any star clients—producers, directors, actors—who would be willing to go onto a BBC program the following Sunday to be interviewed on the subject of a prospective change in the UK tax law affecting the foreign community. The Labor government was working to substantially change the taxation on the foreign domiciled community living and working in the UK in an adverse way. But Irwin expressed his regrets to those people at the BBC, for he had no one that he could get at this short notice who would be willing and able to be interviewed on the matter. Until, all of a sudden, Linda Lovelace was sitting before him, the most famous pornography star in the world (and arguably of all time). Lovelace was telling Irwin how she was in the UK to go to Ascot and mingle with the crowd and promote her now-very-successful film *Deep Throat*. But as she was thinking about moving to this side of the pond, she was also curious to know as much as she could about the rumor of these changes to the UK tax law affecting the foreign community. Was it true? If it were, this would greatly impact her decision on whether or not to move here in the first place. She was very interested to know as much as she could about the matter. This being the case, we asked Lovelace whether she would like some free publicity. Yes, she could appear on the BBC the following Sunday to be interviewed and discuss the changes to the tax law in the UK and how these changes might affect her decision on whether or not to move to London at all. To which she said that, of course, she would love to talk about all of the above—*and more*—on the BBC. Publicity was one of the very reasons she was in the UK and in *our* offices.

I was appointed the task of calling the BBC and giving them the good news, which I happily did. To be sure, there was a certain kind of pleasure for a person in my junior position to call up the BBC to tell them I could now offer Linda Lovelace to participate in an interview. I believe the gentleman on the other end of the line dropped the receiver. He may or may not have also been panting. But in any event, the BBC was delighted about Lovelace. And as far as where to conduct the interview, the BBC had decided that they would like to use as their backdrop a well-known site in the American expat community: a bench right beside the American baseball game that was played every Sunday in Hyde Park. (This set was also the backdrop of the Glenda Jackson and George Segal film, *A Touch of Class*.) The game fielded many people from CBS and the American media at large. Lovelace was more than happy about the choice of location. I had been placed in charge of making sure she arrived for the interview. (It was also determined that I would participate *in* the interview, being an expert on the subject. But more on that momentarily.) I could already imagine all the heads that would be turning and all the people in Hyde Park who would be wondering who this chap was with Linda Lovelace. I rather looked forward to that. However, I did have one issue of concern to me. Though happy to pick up Linda Lovelace and bring her to Hyde Park, I was by this time separated from my first wife, and it was my weekend to be with our four-year-old daughter, Katherine. Despite all my efforts, I could not find a babysitter. It is the plot of a Hollywood film, isn't it? A man goes to pick up the most famous pornography actress in the world to bring her to a very professional interview, but he can't find anyone to watch his young daughter and so he must bring her along. But first I had to ask Linda whether she was comfortable with me having my daughter in tow for the day. If she wasn't, I did not know what I would have done. But to my great relief, Linda, a most gracious person, said not only would she be happy to have my daughter along for the interview, she would like to have us to breakfast at the hotel beforehand. I was relieved. And now those who saw Linda demurely walking through Hyde Park with this chap and a young girl would have to think something entirely different. For instance, that we were a family. Regardless, there was business to attend to. We had an interview with the BBC.

My daughter and I met Linda at the Four Seasons Hotel where she was staying while in London. We had breakfast in the dining room there. Linda was very conservatively dressed, and we had a very pleasant time. To be sure, I was worried about my daughter going home to her mother and being asked what she had done over the weekend and her having to reply:

"Oh Mom, Dad and I had such a lovely time with Linda Lovelace."

"No, you didn't. That's not possible."

"Yes, Mom, Linda Lovelace. You know, the one from *Deep Throat*."

"Honey, please! That's impossible."

Afterward, we went to Hyde Park for the interview with the BBC. While the filming was underway, my daughter enjoyed herself on a nearby swing, and Linda Lovelace and I fielded one question after another from the BBC correspondent. As I much expected, all of my screentime, my knowledgeable answers on the matter of taxation on the foreign domiciled community, ended up on the proverbial cutting room floor. Yes, every moment was Lovelace's. Who could blame the BBC? She was the one everyone was just dying to lay eyes on. She was the reason everyone was tuning in in the first place. And *she* was the reason that *I* was even there—and so I could hardly be all that disappointed. Furthermore, I had spent this incredible day with one of the most famous women in the world and my daughter, the three of us together, in wonderful spirits. Who could really ask for anything more?

I did not see Linda Lovelace again after this experience. But some five years later, I received a call from Linda's ex-husband, Chuck Traynor. By this time, I had left Margulies and Sterling and begun my own firm. Traynor introduced himself and said that he was now married to the actress and adult film star Marilyn Chambers, and that she had been asked to do a show called *Sex Confessions* at Paul Raymond's Boulevard Theater. (Raymond was a very well-known Soho property owner and London "adult entertainment" impresario.) Traynor explained that Marilyn was concerned about her tax liabilities under UK rules. She had also been asked to write a weekly article for one of the major newspapers and had been given a contract to sign. Traynor had been told that I knew something about dealing with these matters and that he was happier dealing with these issues with an American. Could I help him? I told him that I could certainly do the tax side and that I could also look at the contract Marilyn had been tendered for the writing of the newspaper column. Traynor suggested that I come down to the Boulevard Theater, take in one of Marilyn's performances, and that we could have a conversation after the show about Marilyn's tax exposures and newspaper contract. I said that this sounded fine, and Traynor sent me a ticket.

I went to the opening night performance of *Sex Confessions*. A description of the show as performed the previous year in Las Vegas, at the time called *Sex Surrogate*, survives on the packaging of the video in which it would later be sold:

"[This] was the first totally nude stage presentation allowed in Las Vegas. The city attorney justified the one-woman show on the grounds that it was of 'socially redeeming value.' Originally scheduled for a limited engagement, the show was held over, due to public and critical acclaim as well as standing-room only audiences. [It] is the story of a dedicated female psychologist and sex surrogate who explores some of the sexual problems that plague contemporary men and women."

Now, it should be said that Marilyn Chambers, despite the fact that everyone generally wanted to write her off as *just* a pornographic film star, was a true actress. She had had roles in several major features, including the Barbra Streisand film, *The Owl and the Pussycat*, and David Cronenberg's debut, *Rabid*. She had done a lot of theater, including a role in Neil Simon's *Last of the Red Hot Lovers*. And, she had come on the scene as the beautiful young mother cradling a little baby in an Ivory Soap commercial. "99.44% pure," went the slogan. She was even on the soap box and became famous for this. In large part, what Marilyn had done afterward, as far as her pornography career, had been a very intelligent way of subverting this idea of the *pure* maternal figure on a soap box. This was another instance where the pornography world merged with the mainstream media—and, like Linda Lovelace,

Marilyn had been instrumental in breaking these cultural grounds.

So, taking my seat that night in the sold-out Boulevard Theater, there was every reason to give Marilyn credit for doing the show. She had even written the whole one-act performance that I was about to see. As with *Sex Surrogate* before it, she played a psychoanalyst, interviewing three men. One was the typical uptight English accountant with spectacles; the second was a swashbuckling Texan replete with cowboy hat and boots; and the third was a suave Italian lover. Marilyn played all three of these parts *plus* herself, a very funny and extremely clever decision. In order to do this, she would go backstage for a moment and quickly change costumes, now looking like the uptight accountant, now the swashbuckling Texan, and now the suave Italian lover with wild black hair. At the conclusion of the performance, Marilyn ended up completely nude on the stage. Unsurprisingly, the crowd was very pleased. As for me, having had quite the introduction to Marilyn, it was now time to go backstage and discuss business with her and Chuck Traynor. Marilyn would need a few extra minutes, presumably to gather herself after such an arduous performance—and so I first spoke with Chuck about how I could help them negotiate with Inland Revenue on their tax liabilities. We were deep in conversation, when, all of a sudden, Marilyn came backstage to join us and sat down. She was completely nude. No robe, no shirt, no pants, *nothing* at all. I cannot recall any other meetings before or since where any of my clients chose to conduct business in the nude. But with Marilyn, here at the Boulevard Theater, it kind of worked. Marilyn had plenty to say on the subjects at hand, and our conversation led to a proper engagement as their lawyer. I can say that as far as her tax liabilities in the UK and her contract with the British publication, things worked out quite well for her.

But two months later, with *Sex Surrogate* still in performance, I received a panicked phone call from Chuck Traynor. He reminded me that he had been previously married to Linda Lovelace and that they had had quite a stormy relationship. He continued by telling me that Linda, a few years after doing the film *Deep Throat*, had had a "Come to Jesus" moment and had become an Evangelical Christian. Part of that conversion, he said, involved her blaming him for luring her into prostitution and pornography. And now—*now* she had written a book, *Ordeal*, that had been released in the US and was soon to be published in the UK. A two-page spread had recently been printed in a British newspaper about Traynor, their marriage, and the book that Lovelace had written. Traynor was furious because he said that much of this book was fictional, created explicitly to give justification for her conversion to Evangelical Christianity. Traynor needed me, for he was prepared to go after the newspaper and sue them for libel because what they had printed, what had been alleged, he stated, was preposterous. I said that okay, we would take a look at it.

Libel damages in the UK are nothing like the awards that are given in the United States. But in any event, I spoke to a colleague, Peter Carter-Ruck, who was a top libel lawyer in London. I explained the situation to him and that we had to decide whether or not to proceed and bring action against the newspaper for printing what was allegedly a false description of a marital relationship, including allegations of assault and battery, and a fictional description by design. Now that alone would have been grounds for a libel action in the UK. There was no protection, as there was in the United States, through the landmark libel action of *The New York Times v. Sullivan*, which permitted mistakes to be made in written allegations as long as they were not with malice a forethought, meaning that the statement could not have been made with knowledge that it was false or expressed with a reckless disregard for the truth. In the UK, it is very simple: it is a question of fact. A statement can be libelous if it is inaccurate.

Peter and I both read Lovelace's book. The allegations were in a major newspaper in London, and to bring litigation would stir up a lot of press and attention. So, we really had to think this through. And, after reading the book, Peter and I had the same reaction: the book was trashy, it was poorly written, lacking a good story, and if we were to bring an action, all we would do was massively increase the sales for this otherwise unattractive and inconsequential book. Therefore, the best thing that Traynor could do—the best advice from not one but *two* lawyers was the rarely heard advice: *don't sue!*

The book did not deserve bringing an action at all. Traynor would be best served if he allowed the book to vanish on its own, which was exactly what would happen if the flames of its publicity were not fanned. Traynor agreed that this would be the most sensible path, and he did not push us to bring an action. And, as we anticipated, at least in the UK, Lovelace's book disappeared shortly after, with very poor sales. A non-issue. Or so we thought at the time. In fact, the alleged abuse Linda suffered over her married life with Chuck Traynor has been the subject of several articles strongly suggesting an abusive relationship, including an *MS* magazine article by Gloria Steinem in 1980. A film about the alleged abusive relationship, *Lovelace*, was produced in 2013. Not suing for libel did seem to have been a wise decision.

Chuck Traynor and Marilyn Chambers took off for California after the closing of her show at the Boulevard Theater, and I never saw them again. Much has been said about the relationship between Chuck Traynor and his first wife, Linda Lovelace. I can only say that my relationship with Chuck Traynor and his second wife, Marilyn Chambers, was quite appropriate, professional, and that I do not have a view on which part, if any, of the Lovelace/Traynor story has merit. Linda Lovelace and I got on very well, and Traynor and Chambers were fine clients who paid their bills on time and had been very thoughtful about how we approached different issues. But by bringing me on to help them work through some of their issues in the UK, my place in the Linda Lovelace-Chuck Traynor-Marilyn Chambers triumvirate had been crystalized, a distinction that is mine alone and borne by no other: yes, I am the only person who can claim to have represented Linda Lovelace, Chuck Traynor, and Marilyn Chambers.

Libel Cases of Note

I believe it is important to share some of the other libel cases in which I convinced a client to do the unthinkable: that is, *not* to sue.

JACKIE COLLINS, THE "WELL-KNOWN TRANSVESTITE"

In the time that I was with Margulies and Sterling, a call came into Irwin Margulies from Oscar Lerman, one of the owners of the famous club Tramp, then probably the hottest of all the nightclubs in London in the 1970s. Lerman was married to the hugely successful author, Jackie Collins, sister of the well-known actress, Joan Collins. Lerman explained to Irwin that his dear wife had been described by *Pageant* magazine, which was a monthly publication based out of California, as the "well-known transvestite, Jackie Collins." Lerman was furious. There was, of course, no truth to the statement. It was, in his words, blasphemous and libelous, and he had determined that he would like to sue *Pageant* magazine for a fortune, for how could they possibly say this about his lovely wife?

The Margulies and Sterling office had a relationship with a famous entertainment firm in California called Wyman, Bautzer, Rothman & Kuchel, and we jointly looked at the possibility of bringing an action against *Pageant* magazine for libel. It was believed that the circumstances were libel *per se*, which means that it was automatic, the language having impugned the character of a person so thoroughly. (This was the early '70s.) However, again, looking at the matter dispassionately as lawyers, not only could we not prove damages from the magazine having called Jackie Collins a "well-known transvestite," but, in fact, in the weeks after *Pageant* magazine ran its article, sales of Collins's books shot up. (As the old adage in the industry goes: any publicity is good publicity. And in this case, the publicity was hurting our case because it was helping Collins sell books.) Therefore, despite the desires of Jackie Collins and Oscar Lerman to get even with *Pageant* magazine, we discouraged them from suing. Perhaps a personal sense of satisfaction would come of doing so, but they would not be rewarded with any damages, and the whole action would be a waste of money.

After hearing our arguments, Lerman agreed, and we did not sue. As a token of his appreciation— and his having been especially pleased to work with lawyers who did not just automatically tell him to go ahead and sue—Lehrman gave lifetime club memberships to Tramp to me and to the associate I had working with me on the matter. All of these years later, our memberships are still active. We pay twenty-five pounds a year as our membership dues. And though I haven't been there in a long, long time, in the club's heyday I was there often, and what a wonderful scene it was.

Douglas Fairbanks Jr.
and the Duchess of Argyll's Book of Lovers

One day, the prominent actor, Douglas Fairbanks Jr., came to me because he had on good authority that someone was writing a book about a quite infamous woman in London, Margaret Campbell, the duchess of Argyll, also known as "the Dirty Duchess." As it were, some twenty-five years earlier, the duchess's second husband, Ian Douglas Campbell, the eleventh duke of Argyll, had discovered compromising Polaroids of her with another man and soon after brought a hugely public divorce proceeding against his wife. The duke of Argyll claimed that his wife had had relations with eighty-eight men during the course of their marriage. However, it was the man in the Polaroid, who became known to the media as the "headless man," that was of concern to Douglas Fairbanks Jr. and why he was requesting my services.

No one knew the identity of the "headless man" in the Polaroid. At the time of the divorce between the duke and duchess of Argyll, all of London was speculating on whether it was one man or another. It was the hottest gossip in town. Despite all of the names that had been considered possible matches for the "headless man," no one had determined just who it was. One of the possible culprits happened to be Douglas Fairbanks Jr. What concerned Fairbanks, however, was a new book that was about to be published on the subject of the "headless man." Fairbanks feared that he could end up being accused of being the unknown man. The sheer possibility of such an allegation was very upsetting to him. His wife, who was then battling a serious illness, could be especially unhappy to learn of his alleged philandering. Fairbanks was considering bringing an action against the book to stop it from being published.

From a legal standpoint, this was a tough one. We didn't know whether or not to bring an action. Given the normal limitations on the ability to stop publications before they became part of the public marketplace, it was unclear how much we could do. What we decided, once again, was that it did not make sense to bring an action. For one thing, what if the book did not accuse him of being the "headless man" in the first place? Or, what if his wife, who was not long for this world and whose heart he was trying to spare, passed away before the book even came out? (At his late age, Fairbanks seemed not to care in the least about how the book would affect his own reputation.) Moreover, suing might appear to be some kind of admission of guilt. So, we brought no action, and it turned out, once again, to be the right decision, as nothing happened as a result of the book, and Fairbanks was very appreciative.

THE YALE PROFESSOR VS. THE BRITISH MP

While with Morgan Lewis, I was approached by a professor of history from Yale University, who was on leave from Yale for a year and teaching at a London university. As has already been mentioned, I was a graduate of the school. (I was also former president of the Yale Club of London for fourteen years and had done quite a lot of interviewing students in the UK who wished to attend school in

New Haven.) Yale University got a hold of me and asked if I could help a professor in London who was coming up against a very difficult legal situation. He was being sued by a member of Parliament for libel. On what basis? The professor had done a very scholarly history on the Indian and Pakistani battle over the splitting up of the two nations. But one of the very-hard-to-find footnotes in this scholarly work referred to a *Times of New Delhi* newspaper article in 1948, which was quoted as saying that such and such individual, now a member of Parliament in the UK, was an "ardent Communist." This MP was so upset about having found himself referred to in this manner in this very-difficult-to-find footnote in this little-read scholarly work that he had decided to sue the author of the book, this Yale professor currently working in the UK.

Of course, in the US, this case would have been thrown out of court immediately. But again, in the UK, the motive as to why something has appeared in print has no such bearing on the determination of whether or not something is libelous. If the statement is inaccurate, it is subject to a libel action. Therefore, this unfortunate professor was being sued and he needed help. Yale covered his legal expenses, which made matters slightly more palatable for him, and the professor conceded that this was his footnote from a New Delhi newspaper in 1948. He certainly did not deny it. This was not even *his* allegation that the MP was an "ardent Communist." He was merely quoting a newspaper. Either way, our view was that the professor should simply concede the point, give the MP one hundred pounds, and let the case vanish altogether. And that is what happened.

CHAPTER SIX

Michael Jackson Has a Case of Beatlemania

One day in the early 1980s, John Branca, the prominent entertainment lawyer who's represented everyone from Fleetwood Mac to The Rolling Stones, The Beach Boys, Carlos Santana, and numerous others, called me up from his office in California. We had no prior business relationship whatsoever, but John wanted to know if I could help him on a small matter—the tax liabilities associated with Michael Jackson's upcoming performances in the UK. I don't recall who referred John to me, but by that time I had completed representation of a number of well-known performers, from Diana Ross to Earth, Wind & Fire, as well as John's client, Santana. I told John that I would gladly be of assistance, and I sorted out the matter for him, and that was that.

Some years later, John called me up again. This time, he had a much more serious piece of business for me. Michael Jackson wanted to purchase all the music publishing catalogues owned by Sir Robert Holmes à Court through his company ATV Music, a major music publishing company in the UK. Holmes à Court had been dealing with some financial problems in his home country, Australia, and was prepared to sell the entire group of catalogues, which included Northern Songs Ltd., The Beatles' music publishing catalogue. Jackson had been interested in buying up music publishing catalogues at this time, and The Beatles' catalogue was *the* great prize.

Back in the mid-1980s, music publishing catalogues were certainly valuable, and perhaps none higher than The Beatles' catalogue. But no one could have known the extent to which music publishing catalogues would rise in value in the years to come. At the time of this writing, Paul Simon had just sold his music publishing catalogue for an estimated $250 million, Bob Dylan for an estimated $300 million, and Bruce Springsteen for an estimated $500 million. Music publishing is big business. In the mid-1980s, the numbers were not quite so high, but they were certainly trending up. Jackson, certainly knowledgeable about the music industry but also influenced by John Branca as well as his legendary business manager, Marshall Gelfand, understood that music publishing was a solid investment. Ironically, it was none other than Paul McCartney who had tipped Michael off to its possible availability. The conversation in which McCartney educated Jackson on the subject is now the stuff of legend. Did McCartney convince Jackson to buy The Beatles' catalogue? Perhaps, in a sense, he did. Over an evening together at McCartney's house, Sir Paul riled up the King of Pop with detailed descriptions of all the songs he owned, including those by quite possibly the most important influence on The Beatles themselves, Buddy Holly. McCartney explained the financial sense in owning rock 'n' roll staples and that it was far sexier than owning public stock or real estate. Yes, owning publishing was lucrative *and* attractive.

But first, why didn't McCartney, along with the John Lennon Estate, own The Beatles' publishing catalogue? In fact, a tax issue was to blame. In the late 1960s in the UK, with the tax rate on earned income at 83 percent (and as high as 98 percent on unearned income), McCartney and Lennon could hardly afford to keep their music publishing on their dozens of hit songs. Advised to sell off their copyrights (while retaining the writer's share of the income), Lennon and McCartney sold their publishing company, Northern Songs Ltd. In an unforeseeable twist, the majority stock in that company would soon be bought up by Sir Lew Grade (yes, that Sir Lew Grade, the very one we encountered when discussing my work with Jim Henson and the Muppets) through his company ATV Music. Then, in 1981, Robert Holmes à Court, the Australian businessman, the first billionaire of that nation and what some would call a corporate raider, would acquire ATV, and along with it, The Beatles' publishing catalogue. Holmes à Court could now claim to own the rights to most every Beatles song from "Love Me Do" to "Let It Be." If a song was played on the radio, ATV Music got paid. But also, if any song was going to be used in a film or commercial, or if it was to be covered by another artist, the right to do so would have to be granted by ATV Music. Such is the power vested in the music publishing copyright owner of a song. Naturally, McCartney had always been interested in buying back his portion of The Beatles' publishing catalogue, but for reasons unknown to the public, he had not.

Enter Michael Jackson.

After his conversation with McCartney, Jackson asked John Branca to pursue buying some music publishing catalogues. What was out there on the market? Whose catalogues? Jackson wanted to know. But it was especially important to Jackson that he have a relationship *to* the music. That is, he wouldn't just buy any publishing catalogues. It was imperative that he loved the music—and The Beatles' music was at the top of his list. When John Branca came to him one day and said that Holmes à Court had put a number of publishing catalogues, including Northern Songs Ltd., on the market, Michael, according to journalist Robert Hilburn in an article in the *LA Times*, "did a full turn, jumped in the air and shrieked."

"Other people are also after the catalogue," Branca was reported saying, according to the same *LA Times* article.

To which Michael replied, "I don't care. I want it."

As so happened, John Branca suggested to me that Holmes à Court had a serious problem. ATV's music publishing companies had written off most of its costs over the years, including writers' advances, and thus royalties projected for the future would be fully taxable in the UK. Moreover, Holmes à Court insisted on selling the companies so he could then repatriate the money tax-free back to Australia to cover his debts. Then, of course, for Jackson, there were US tax problems associated with his being a US citizen. All said, there was a lot of concern about how the deal might be structured so that both Holmes à Court and Jackson could get what they needed to make the deal profitable. I told John Branca that this sounded very intriguing.

I set to work thinking through the complex properties of the deal, talking to various people, including ATV, about how the deal might be structured. But, as Hilburn explained in the *LA Times*, "Negotiations became so snarled in May [of 1985] that Michael's representatives walked away from the talks and refused calls for nearly a month—even though they'd already spent more than $1 million and hundreds of hours in their quest to realize Michael's dream of owning The Beatles' music."

Honestly, it looked to me like the deal wasn't going to go through. I even went off on holiday with my family to Italy. We were scheduled to spend a month in the hills outside of Florence and had really been looking forward to the time away. But then all of a sudden, I received an urgent call from John Branca's partner, Gary Stiffelman. It was already evening, and I had not been expecting to hear from Stiffelman, but he explained that the deal was heating back up and that I had to return to London at once, for there was a lot to work to do and no time to waste. I had to catch a 3:00 a.m. train from Florence to Rome and then get on an airplane to London so that we could get right to work. It was so early in the morning that I had to dodge the milk-maids. Getting to the train station at that hour in Italy, during the summer, when nothing was open, was very difficult. And then to get to the airport in Rome, fly to London, go straight to the office—it was all a big to-do. But for a deal like this, with an artist like Michael Jackson at the peak of his success, you do what you must.

It took a lot of thinking to get the deal right—Stiffelman would claim to have spent nine hundred hours on this deal, it was so complicated—but we came up with a solution that was unique and doable at that time (though it wouldn't work today due to changes in the tax law both in the US as well as in the UK). But we developed an ingenious solution. We bought all the shares of the ATV music publishing companies for a cost of $47.5 million. Then we moved the residence of the companies from the UK to the Bahamas by changing the directors and changing the way in which the companies operated. Jackson, through the non-UK independent directors, ran the companies for six months or thereabouts in the Bahamas, and then we liquidated the compa-nies into Jackson's personal hands. Because we were running the companies as Bahamian companies where we didn't receive any tax treaty protection, there was a relatively minor tax issue having to do with withholding tax on the royalties in that interim period of six months. To my knowledge, neither the IRS, nor the Inland Revenue in the UK, had any issues beyond that. And then a couple of years later, Jackson would put his catalogues into a joint venture with Sony. This was an interesting exercise. My team was responsible for the non-US part of the joint venture, essentially ensuring that the new structure was treated as a partnership for US tax purposes so that Jackson could get a foreign tax credit for any foreign taxes paid on the non-US royalties.

The result of all of this effort was:

1) Holmes à Court got what he wanted, which was the sale of the shares of the music publishing companies. This was very important to him because it allowed Holmes à Court to move the money back to Australia and pay off a lot of debt.

2) Jackson got what's called a step-up in basis to the fair market value of all of the copyrights that he bought. This meant that Jackson paid $47.5 million, and he had a depreciable asset of close to $47 million (the actual copyright value), that he could then amortize over a certain number of years against the income that came from the catalogues. This effectively meant that he could pay all of the interest and some of the capital costs for financing the entire transaction with tax-deductible dollars. So, if I might say

so, it was a brilliant strategy because, effectively, Jackson could pay for the catalogues with pre-tax money.

It is well-known that McCartney was furious about Michael buying up The Beatles' publishing catalogue, especially after McCartney had been the one to tell him why it would be such a valuable investment. Though the two had had a hit with their duet, "Say Say Say," just two years prior in 1983, the friendship was officially over. But there is a larger truth that McCartney was not confronting in the deal: Michael could afford to pay more than McCartney for the copyrights to The Beatles' songs. Because McCartney was living in the UK, he would have had to pay tax on all of the income of The Beatles' publishing catalogue as it was earned in the companies. Then those companies would have declared a dividend, and McCartney, if he had financed the acquisition, would have had to pay his tax on his dividends and then pay interest and principal to the banks or whomever had financed his purchase. Effectively, we had bought The Beatles' publishing catalogue with pre-tax money, and McCartney would have had to buy the catalogue with post-tax money. Or, as we say, the difference between chicken shit and chicken salad.

"Michael Jackson's $47.5 million purchase of The Beatles' song collection last month was the climax of 10 months of intense, complicated and confusing on-again, off-again negotiations. The package—of which the Beatles music was only part of the nearly 4,000-song ATV Music catalogue—is believed to be the most expensive publishing purchase ever by an individual," wrote Hilburn in the *LA Times*.

During the protracted negotiation, I did have the opportunity to meet Jackson in person. I received a call from John Branca saying that Jackson was in town for the unveiling of his wax statue at Madame Tussaud's and staying at the Montcalm Hotel. Why not introduce him to the seller? I said sure, of course, let's introduce them.

I called up the lawyers and frightened them a little bit, saying that we had a problem with the deal and that I was worried that it might crater, and so I wanted to set up a meeting in my office at such and such a time to talk. Sure enough, they showed up at my offices ready to talk about problems with the deal—whereupon Jackson joined the meeting, having snuck out the back door of his hotel unbeknownst to the thousands of his adoring fans who had been waiting out front for him. Dressed in his famous silver iridescent suit and with his driver the only member of his entourage at his side, Jackson arrived at my office in St. James. Needless to say, everyone was in awe of him. Jackson's first reaction to the contract was that there was a lot of paper.

"Yes, Michael, it's a complicated deal," I said.

And he reckoned that it was.

One bit of irony: the meeting with Jackson, as well as some of the other negotiations in the minefield of protracted and difficult negotiations, took place in the Morgan Lewis conference room at 4 Carlton Gardens, the very room that General Charles de Gaulle used as his office as the headquarters of the Free French during the German occupation of France in World War II.

We went through a few elements of the transaction, making sure Jackson was comfortable meeting the seller, and then we dismissed the lawyers and talked to Jackson separately. And to his credit, Jackson understood the guts of the transaction. He knew what it meant to buy and to exploit copyrights. He had a good sense of the big picture of this deal. As a result, when the hard decisions had to be made—for instance, how much were we going to pay in the end; what was the basis of doing the transaction—he could do that kind of thinking, despite it being a complicated transaction that required a lot of legal skill. And that's saying a lot for him or anyone. Buying publishing catalogues *is* complicated. For one thing, you have to make sure you really own the copyrights to the titles. "You can't just assume all the papers and copyrights are in order even though ATV has been involved with them for years," Branca told the *LA Times* reporter Hilburn. "What if it turned out that Lennon and McCartney signed a contract that gave away rights after, say, thirty years to several key songs?" And for another, you have to get a sense of the value of the copyrights based on the copyright period that is still available. What are the laws governing the life of a copyright in each territory? Jackson could make sense of all this information. This was not just a lawyer's deal; it was *Jackson's* deal, and he had earned it.

The final piece of the deal was quite entertaining. After all the back and forth, the delaying, the gamesmanship, Holmes à Court had one last request: yes, he said to Jackson that he was prepared to finalize the deal, but that he would like one last thing. His daughter, Catherine, was in love with The Beatles' catalogue. Perhaps she imagined that she would one day inherit it. Regardless, Holmes à Court said that it would be such a nice gesture and allow him to finally close the deal if Jackson were able to give Catherine *just one* Beatles copyright. He assured Jackson that he wouldn't have to worry about the income-side, that Jackson would receive a good enough management fee for the copyright so that he wouldn't feel that he was being taken advantage of financially, but that it would really be a nice gesture if Catherine could choose the copyright of her favorite song. The song Holmes à Court's daughter, Catherine, had in mind wasn't "Let It Be," nor "Yesterday," but "Penny Lane." And Michael, no doubt desperate to have the deal signed and happy enough with his haul of Beatles tunes, agreed and the deal was signed. But then wouldn't you know it, "Penny Lane" had at the time of the closing the highest NPS ("Net Publisher's Share") of all The Beatles' songs to date.

CHAPTER SEVEN
Coke Dinner

I received a phone call one Friday morning in 1974 while working at the law practice of Margulies and Sterling. A young woman was on the line.

"Hello," she said, "my name is Sharon. I've been referred to you by a Phil *X* in California. He tells me that you know how to get rid of some snow."

I said, "I beg your pardon." It was early, but I was not dreaming. No, I was wide awake and quite certain that I had understood this young woman correctly. Then she confirmed as much.

"Yes, Phil told me that you're an American in London and that you know your way *around* and that you know how to get rid of some snow."

Well, there it was, the confirmation that I *had* understood her. Sitting up in my chair, crossing one leg over the other, clearing my throat, I explained to her that there had been a gross misunderstanding and that despite what she had heard, I had no inroads whatsoever in the kind of business that she was referring to.

"Sorry I can't be of any help."

However, there was something about this young woman, Sharon. She sounded so charming, so delightful. I was not prepared to hang up the phone just then and let that be the end of things. Perhaps I detected in her a kind of kinship, an adventurous spirit born out of her original query as to whether I had connections in the sale of cocaine. Who can say, really? But now I was up on my feet, leaning over my wooden desk, determined to ask her out. It just so happened that I was going to an art opening in Central London that night, and I proposed that she join me and we get acquainted. Sharon told me that she just so happened to be free that evening and she would love to accompany me.

Sharon was twenty-four years old, a petite, beautiful black-haired young woman, and a very spiritual Californian. Perhaps some of her energetic qualities were being urged on by the aforementioned *snow*. Either way, we hit it off at once. I identified a similarity between the two of us. She was clearly adventurous and a risk taker. I could tell this about her before we had even left the art exhibition, which turned out to be pretty bad. I suggested that the two of us go off to have some dinner, and Sharon said she would love to. I made reservations at a well-known private club in the entertainment world of 1970s London, the White Elephant, and off we went. At the White Elephant, we continued to enjoy ourselves. We had our starter, we had our main course, and then I suggested some dessert. Her response was immediate. "Before any sweets, why don't you try some of this first?" Whereupon, from across the table in this elegant London restaurant, Sharon took a coke spoon off her neck, dabbed a small bump of white powder into it, reached out her slender arm, bringing the spoon beneath my nose. Then she smiled her gorgeous smile and said, "Go on. You know, for dessert."

This was the first time I had ever tried cocaine, and it was probably better than anything on the menu. Suddenly, a random phone call on a Sunday morning, the pleasure I had taken in the quality of the caller's voice, the nervy decision to act on a feeling and ask this caller out, had brought me to this very high and unexpected place. I could not have been happier.

Though Sharon was in London *on business*, she was planning a trip for the upcoming weeks that would take her to Mauritius and the Seychelles Islands, both off the east coast of Africa in the Indian Ocean. I told her that this was truly coincidental, because if she were to visit these places, she would likely have to go through Kenya, and I actually had a trip scheduled there for the elections of 1974 because my business partner was running for parliament. I suggested that I go my own way to Kenya and that we meet one another there and head off to Mauritius and the Seychelles together. We were only on our second date when we coordinated these quite ambitious travels, but Sharon was a very spirited lass and willing to take such a risk—and she thought this adventurous trip with a near stranger sounded like a wonderful idea.

Speaking of *risk*, did I mention that Sharon was in fact a professional cocaine smuggler? When I found this out, I had already committed to our trip to Kenya and Mauritius and the Seychelles. But that did not change my travel plans. Discovering that Sharon, this beautiful young woman, *also* spent time in the mountains of Bolivia negotiating for cocaine with the natives there, I was all the more compelled to pack my bags and head out on this jaunt with her. Honestly, my attraction to her only deepened when I learned that she sold cocaine for a few months of the year and then did her photography (she was a skilled photographer). skied for several months, and spent the rest of the years in a little house outside LA. What guts. What chutzpah. Compared to all the other relationships in my life, whether romantic or otherwise, this was entirely unique, with someone truly original. Call it exotic. I was smitten.

We headed off on our journey, and Sharon met me in Kenya, where I had arrived several days earlier. Spirits were especially high because my business partner had won the election to parliament. Unfortunately, however, I could not stick around and celebrate his victory as much as I may have liked, as Sharon and I were off to the islands. It's not a short trip to that part of the world, but what a beautiful part of the world it is, so remote, so enchanting. It was a fascinating experience for me, mainly because in the bottom of Sharon's purse at the start of our travels was as much as sixteen ounces of pure cocaine. And when I say pure, I mean *pure*. When it came out of the Bolivian jungles, it was 95 percent pure and it *stayed* that pure. And how do I know that? Well, the DEA would later tell us. (But more on that soon.)

Perhaps it comes as no surprise to hear that I was fairly innocent at that time. Obviously, I knew that Sharon was carrying something, but I had no idea that she was so well connected in the drug-smuggling profession and that she had so much cocaine. And then I realized why she wanted so many stamps in her passport, which was one of the reasons for taking this East African and Indian Ocean trip. I was blinkered, as they say. I was along for the ride, so to speak. We were having such a great time on the islands. Going from village to village, from beach to beach, and I was being exposed to something that I had never tasted before. It was an exquisite time, as ideal as any.

Eventually, we had to come home from paradise—me to my London law practice and Sharon to her next adventure—and at least temporarily part ways. Sharon returned to London, stayed with me for a few weeks, eventually going back to the States and her primary market. But then upon landing at Dulles Airport in Northern Virginia, she was examined. Why they would examine Sharon of all people, who's to say? A single woman traveling on her own and being spirited and beautiful could be grounds for a search. But what they found was more than a few twigs of marijuana. Sure enough, she was carrying eight ounces of pure cocaine *into* the United States. She was stopped by the feds. In that part of the world at that time—Northern Virginia in 1974—having cocaine on your person was bad enough. However, bringing cocaine into the country for the purposes of selling it was very serious. They arrested Sharon and jailed her. She was indicted both for intent to import cocaine *and* also intent to import with the intent to distribute. Both of these felonies could mean five to fifteen years in prison. Sharon had big problems on her hands, and she needed my help.

As soon as I knew she had been incarcerated, I made an urgent call to a very close friend who was a top white-collar litigator in Washington, D.C., Tom Green. I explained the circumstances and said that I really needed his help. He asked me if I cared for Sharon. And when I told him that I did, he began to lay out a plan for how we could improve her situation. For all of Sharon's peripatetic life, she did have a permanent home in a small, rented house just outside LA. My friend suggested that we bring a motion to "change the venue" on grounds of *forum non conveniens*. That is, we could move the trial from the Federal District Court in Northern Virginia, where for this kind of charge judges generally put you in jail and threw away the key, to the Southern District of California where, by and large, there was much more understanding shown to people like Sharon.

And we went ahead with this plan, making a motion to the judge and explaining that Sharon really had no contact whatsoever with Northern Virginia, unless one were to make a big deal of the fact that she happened to be aboard an aircraft that landed there. To our great relief, the judge honored the motion, and the venue was moved to the Southern District of California. At this point, Sharon brought in a proper drug lawyer. She would plead guilty to the charge of intent to import if they would drop the charge of the intent to import with intent to distribute. It wasn't too much to ask. After all, wasn't it reasonable to view eight ounces of cocaine as being for one to use for one's own recreational purposes, say, among friends, rather than as an amount to be used for the earning of a living? Sharon pled guilty, with her drug lawyer there at her side. But there was an issue, one that threatened to torpedo her hopes of a plea bargain. The thing was, Sharon had a record. A probation report showed that at the precocious age of fourteen, she had brought back into the United States two kilos of hashish from Lebanon. What an ambitious young girl she had been, to already have been on the professional track. Those two kilos of hashish had been a problem then—and they were a problem now. Sharon had a track record. We were all deeply concerned for her. She went to sentencing. The drug lawyer got up and began to tell the story of her life to the judge. It was a serviceable performance. But then Sharon stood up and asked her lawyer to please stop and to step aside, for she would like to speak for herself to the judge. And so there came Sharon, this pint-sized, beautiful twenty-four-year-old Californian cocaine dealer talking to this elderly judge in the Southern District of California Court. Steeling herself, calling upon all her strength, she told the judge that she had lived all over the world and that in those places people...well...they took drugs. Yes, they did. It was part of the culture. They didn't think it was so strange, and they certainly did not find it a criminal act. She asked the judge if he wanted to be responsible for jailing a twenty-four-year-old girl just because she had a small amount of drugs on her? Tears were streaming down her face as she pled. Being in a part of the world, the Southern District of California Court, where drugs were not only seen as less reprehensible but also great performances could go highly rewarded, the judge gave Sharon a pass: a two-year suspended sentence. She was free to go.

We were all thrilled by the ruling. Released from custody, Sharon could now travel back to London to her conservative law-abiding boyfriend. She remained with me for about two weeks, when she then shot off to Southern Argentina with her ski instructor. That had not been my plan, nor my hope. But what could I do about it? A person like Sharon could not be contained. I did not see her for a year. I didn't know what had even happened to her. I spoke to her friends in California. No one knew anything. There were rumors that the IRS was chasing her from her original home in Hawaii and that she had changed partners and was traveling in the Midwest. But that was all rumor and hearsay. I really didn't know what the true story was. Nevertheless, I wondered about her often. Would I ever see her again? Was that it for us?

Then a year later, I received a call from Sharon. I was already living with my current wife, Dominique, by then. But Sharon said that she was in London and that she wanted to see me. I told her that I would be happy to see her, but that I hoped she had given up that exotic trade that she had been pursuing. To which she replied that she would tell me what trade she was currently doing when she saw me. And, to the consternation of Dominique, who would have preferred that I cut ties with Sharon altogether, I went off into the night to meet her. My feelings were no longer there for Sharon. It all felt like a long time ago now. I just wanted to check in with Sharon, have some closure. She told me that she had greatly cleaned up her act. She was somewhat vague about how, but I took her at her word. She then disappeared from London, and I never saw her again. However, about a month later, I got a letter in the mail with one ounce of 95 percent pure cocaine. No note, no nothing. Just the cocaine in the envelope. (Of course, I was a little concerned because I could recall that Jerry Hall had recently received the same kind of package in the Caribbean, and it had caused her no end of grief.) But I didn't have any kind of grief whatsoever. Quite to the contrary, my wife and I enjoyed the present, and Sharon went out of my life for good on the same wonderful buzz on which she had come in.

*   *   *

The time between Sharon being released from custody and her ultimate appearance before her sentencing was a significant portion of 1974. I took a couple of trips to the States in that time, and I managed to see Sharon. On one of those occasions, we spent a couple of weeks together in California, where I stayed at her place. But she also accompanied me to St. Louis where I was negotiating for a businessman by the name of Felix Pole—a very successful property developer in the United Kingdom. But he was also a fascinating character who lived life on the edge. One of his edges was scuba diving in the Bay of Navarino in Greece. During one of his trips as a scuba diver, he found some coins dangling in the water which turned out to have come from a flagship Turkish vessel in the Battle of Navarino Bay in the Greek War of Independence back in the 1820s. These coins were part of a cache of Austrian silver thalers that was worth approximately $20 million. Pole decided that he would pursue this ship that went down in the Battle of Navarino Bay. He put some money up along with a group of investors, and I went to St. Louis to talk to one of these investors. Unfortunately, the investor came into town about a day or so early, I was with Sharon, and let's just say that when he arrived and insisted on seeing me, I was not quite in a position to have a high-level legal conversation on his participation in this particular venture. The investor decided not to participate. Maybe just as well, for Felix, having spoken to the Greek Ministry of Tourism and the Ministry of the Interior, and recognizing that we would have to have a whole host of permissions to go about diving for this shipwreck, was not given legal access to the ship by the Greek government. That is, he was told point blank that the Greek government treated this buried ship, and all its treasures, as a Greek possession and no private person could enter into any of the waters of the Bay of Navarino and search for this shipwreck. But sure enough, the Greek government went down precisely where Felix Pole had told them the ship was located and examined the wreckage and discovered many Austrian silver thalers. Felix, who had done his homework at the British Museum and had found out the entire history of this battle and the lead ship with these many millions of dollars' worth of silver thalers on it—probably there to bribe people to keep the Turks in power in Greece—had not ended up with his bounty in the end. But what an interesting investigation for all of us into the legality of searching the bottom of a nation's seas for what might lay below.

CHAPTER EIGHT

Oh, the People, the Stories

There are experiences from my professional life worth recounting that do not require a full chapter's worth of detail but are nonetheless interesting and unique. I hope you will agree.

Iron Maiden

Iron Maiden, the heavy metal rock band, came to me in the mid-1970s when I was running my small firm. Though they were a UK group formed in Leyton, East London, in 1975, two of the members had permanent residency status in the US—that is, "green cards"—which they had kept when they returned to the UK. Thus, under US tax law, they were taxable on their worldwide income. They all had tax problems, especially the green card holders. But they were seeking my help for reasons beyond their tax issues alone. Indeed, they hoped to do something that belied their heavy metal personae, something which if you watched them on stage—and I did, and they were wild—you might have had a hard time believing. Yes, these men had wives and children and they wanted to plan for their financial futures. In their thirties then, they had all of the solid middle-class desires, in particular, to protect their future with a pension plan and provide for their children's education. Thus, my job was to clean up some of their tax issues and also to help them put together pension plans which worked both in the UK and the United States. I brought in a specialist pension plan firm in the US, and we put together pension plans which, to this day, provide benefits for three of the band's members. To show their gratitude, each year I receive a Christmas card from Iron Maiden with their traditional death-themed cover shots. I have seen them perform a couple of times at the O2 Arena, and they are mesmerizing on stage. But the juxtaposition between their stage personae and their family concerns really struck me. Believe me, throughout all my years, I've had many other clients who were not so responsible.

Bill Graham

Bill Graham, one of the great impresarios of the second half of the twentieth century, was a Holocaust survivor. Born in Berlin in 1931, he and his sister made it out of Germany to France, escaping the Nazi invasion. His sister and brother-in-law stayed in Europe, and Bill went off to the US, where he was raised in a foster home in the Bronx. When he came to me in the late 1970s, I was still running my small independent tax practice and he was already a well-known figure. He had turned the Fillmore West in San Francisco and the Fillmore East in New York into two of the most successful music venues in the country. He had managed Jefferson Airplane, Carlos Santana, and Van Morrison (who Bill got me into a small nightclub in New York to see one evening, a real treat). Bill had even run his own music label. He had an incredibly strong will. You listened to him, or you got out of his way. He really laid down the rules. For instance, with the Rolling Stones, while they were out on a European tour in the time that Bill worked with the band, there were to be no drugs, no drinking, and the members were to be in bed every night at a reasonable hour. Bill took the Stones all over Europe, enforcing a true discipline, and it was a very successful tour. And he got away with controlling them. Mick Jagger is not an easy guy to control, and it is a lasting testament to Bill's skill at his profession. I did a bit of work for him on their tour, and it was impressive to see such normally uncontrollable rock musicians listen to his demands.

But Bill felt obligations to the family that he had left behind in Europe, and he hired me, not so much for my tax expertise, but for other purposes. I helped Bill with some of the property and investment interests he and his family had in Europe. As a US citizen, he had a number of issues that he had to deal with. His issues, however, had to take into account that neither his sister nor his brother-in-law were US citizens. I had to undertake an important role in facilitating support for them and then also extricate his sister from some of the entanglements she had. I saw him many times, both in London and in California.

I was very upset when Bill died aboard a helicopter one night in California. He was really at the pinnacle of his career. It was quite disturbing. I had developed a good working relationship with Bill and a reasonable personal friendship with him over a dozen years—and then he just disappeared.

Albert Finney

Albert Finney was a wonderful actor, and in the early '80s, he had a big US tax problem resulting from work he'd done in films which had been substantially shot in the US. We were asked if there was anything that could be done to reduce his US tax liability. In the past, for clients in such a position, I had found a few investments that were particularly tax efficient. (Others may say that they were tax shelters because of the aggressive manner in which they were applied, but I would disagree.) I put Albert into two investment opportunities. The first concerned the world of horses, which was something he was passionately interested in. It was an investment in a horse-breeding program for the creation of racehorses. Fact was, in the program we designed, one could deduct all the cost of the fertilization in the first year. Eventually, when the colts came out and became racehorses, one might not have to pay tax on the income, depending on where you were a tax resident or where the racing income was earned. Albert was intrigued.

If you are an actor, the year in which you perform your acting services is the year when you need the deductions unless you arrange deferment of some payments. Therefore, if in that same year—1981 or 1982, in Albert's case—you bought into, say, a horse breeding business, you have very large deductions which you can offset against your earned income with the net taxable at 50 percent. Then when the actor went abroad, any deferred payments for his acting services were only subject to a 30 percent withholding tax. And so we did this for Albert Finney: that is, we entered into the breeding structure in year one and deferred some payments into years two and three; he took big losses against his performance income in the US, and when he did receive his deferred payment, he only paid the withholding tax at a 30 percent rate. He was very pleased, as was I. The deferred-payment law was eventually changed by legislation, but some of the accelerated tax benefits for horse breeding are still available.

But the other tax plan for Albert was not so successful. What happened was this: I had a client who had developed a program in which he would buy the residual print runs from a well-known printing group that specialized in modern artists like Claes Oldenburg, Jim Dine, or Mark Rothko. The maker of these prints, Petersburg Press, might do runs of two hundred prints, all signed by the artist, and sell them out to galleries around the country. But, with all print runs, they would keep back, say, fifty or so prints in an edition of two hundred, perhaps because they couldn't get rid of them or because they wanted to keep them as an investment. My client would go in and offer to buy all of the remaining prints. He wouldn't pay a lot for them because Petersburg Press needed the money to do the next print job. They were even happy to sell them for much less than the retail market for an individual print. What my client did was to buy in bulk all these remaining prints from the publisher, Petersburg Press, and then turn around and sell them to US taxpayers at a "reasonable" markup for himself. The US taxpayer would hold the print for a year and would then donate that work of art to a museum or university art gallery somewhere in the US and as identified by my client. This donation was made at the fair market value that the print would sell for in a retail gallery. Effectively, the taxpayers were buying wholesale and donating retail. That could be a difference of four to five times what they had originally paid for the work.

We did this for many clients, and it worked. I thought it was such a good deal that I put my own mother into it. She got through, no problem, without an audit, receiving a general contribution deduction for the same amount that it would be sold in a gallery. The only people who didn't get through were Albert Finney and *me*. Both of us were audited by the IRS. I thought we might go to court, because I viewed ourselves as being on the right side of the law. But we ended up having to settle with the IRS, as the cost of litigation was too much for the amounts involved. The IRS wouldn't give us a full fair market value deduction but would give us the deduction for what we paid and with no penalties.

However, I had another client—a much more aggressive and unstable individual (he enjoyed going into Claridge's with his floor-length mink coat) who thought this method of tax planning was so good that he would do it with Bibles. He bought up an enormous quantity of Bibles and then doled them out to his friends, who would then donate them to their local churches. Perhaps unsurprisingly, this was too much for the IRS and the IRS came down hard with a tough public ruling—a ruling that I still think is probably wrong. The ruling stated that this was an example of a tax shelter that was way too aggressive, and the ruling denied the deduction based on the inability to buy something wholesale and donate it retail. The closing down of that shelter, which had its ramifications on all the work that we had done, meant basically that it could not be replicated in the future. But most of our cases had already gone through the respective tax filings and had all gotten through—again, with the exception of Albert Finney and myself—and so I didn't have to be concerned with what was behind us, only that a door of opportunity had now been closed.

Artists Performing in the UK

Over the years, I have represented many musicians and actors in connection with their performances in the UK, negotiating on their behalf with the Inland Revenue: Harrison Ford (who not only had a UK problem but a French problem, having earned a lot of income in France from services rendered there); Frank Oz; Earth, Wind & Fire; Diana Ross; Santana; Ivo Pogorelîch; Enrique Iglesias; Shirley Bassey; and then Michael Jackson, to name a few. In the early days, before Inland Revenue took an aggressive view on foreign artists, in most cases a performing artist would pay tax on just the salary received through their wholly owned corporations. (Many of the artists performed through their own corporations, essentially so they could have medical and pension plans.) They didn't get much in the way of deferrals, and usually at the end of the year, they would pay out everything through bonuses. We reported the actual individual monthly or quarterly salaries that they had worked out with their business managers, and Inland Revenue rarely challenged this. In fact, one of the revenue agents at Inland Revenue used to take pride in all the artists he had negotiated with, even hanging photos of these performers on his office wall. But then Inland Revenue got wise and, buttressed by a change in the OECD Model tax treaty that specifically targeted performing artists and athletes, overhauled its entire method of taxing these taxpayers, to the great benefit of the UK Exchequer.

As far as the work I did for Michael Jackson in reference to his performances in the UK, on paying his bill, so afraid was he of being ripped off by his agents and representatives, he wrote out his check to me himself (as he did *all* his checks). If I had had a little bit more investor insight, I would have kept that check with the King of Pop's signature on it, never cashed it, and framed it as a memento.

Jean Simmons

One of my favorite films as a teenager was *Spartacus*, and I even recalled the scene in which the heroine [Jean Simmons] was sexually advanced upon during the Roman slave rebellion by Spartacus [Kirk Douglas]. That image was in my head in the mid-'70s when I was asked by Jean Simmons's lawyer to deal with her UK tax affairs while she was performing in *A Little Night Music* in London. She was staying in a suite at the Savoy Hotel, and I went to see her to discuss her tax obligations as a dual US-UK citizen, a non-resident, performing in the UK. I knocked on the door of her suite and was greeted by a tiny lady in socks and a bathrobe. Thinking this was her personal maid, I was about to say, "Would you tell Ms. Simmons that Mr. Lubar is here?" when I halted, and looking directly into those ever so sparkling eyes, I said: "Ms. Simmons?" "Yes," she calmly answered. And I saved myself from a most embarrassing faux pas. She was charming, and her tax issues easily resolved, but I have never forgotten this close call.

Under the Boardwalk, Down by the Sea

I represented a wonderful songwriter, an American who was living in the UK, Kenny Young. He had written many songs, including "Under the Boardwalk," a major hit, originally recorded by The Drifters and later recorded by The Rolling Stones and Bette Midler. But Kenny had the following problem: he lived and worked in the UK, and his total income earned was treated by the Inland Revenue as being derived from his personal services done in the UK. He paid tax on that income as UK source income derived from a UK trade. At the same time, more than 50 percent of that income came from the United States from royalties derived from the exploitation of copyrights there. When he tried to take credit for taxes paid to the United States, the UK said he was not allowed to do so. In their opinion, this was self-employment income generated from inside the UK, and therefore, he was not permitted to take a credit for taxes paid in the US. Reciprocally, the IRS wanted to be paid tax on that income generated inside the US, and they said that he could not take a credit for the UK taxes attributable to his US income, because from their perspective, the income had been earned from inside the US. Fortunately, the Inland Revenue eventually agreed to a tax credit for the taxes paid to the US. I would have gone to court, for the analytical way both governments were looking at the issue would have left Kenny Young with a 98 percent tax.

Sometime later, two things happened to keep situations like Kenny Young's from happening in the future. One, there was a case involving a famous American artist, Mark Tobey, who lived and worked in the UK, which focused on determining whether the artist had "earned income" arising from outside the US (and was thus subject to an exemption from

US tax). The case held that even though he created and sold goods (his artwork), the income was nonetheless "earned income," and he benefitted from the US exemption. That case changed the attitude of the IRS going forward, as the IRS conceded that an artist's or writer's personal efforts generated "earned income" even if he generated copyright royalties or sales of his products (art works). Secondly, in those situations where a US citizen in the UK had income earned—dividends and interest, for example—inside the US but the person was subject nonetheless to full taxation inside the UK, an amendment to the US/UK tax treaty was put in place that allowed the US citizen to "resource" the income to the UK so that the US would give a credit for the UK taxes that were paid on the income derived from the US. With those two changes, Americans living inside the UK were now safe from such egregious situations as Kenny Young had to face.

Japanese Evangelicals

Japanese Evangelicals sounds like a contradiction in terms, but the story is fascinating. At the end of World War II, there were a number of US troops remaining in Japan. One group of seven were friends from the Midwest and children of US missionary families. The families collectively decided that their children should stay in Japan, marry Japanese women, and preach the Gospel to the Japanese. The children did so. To earn a living, they traveled all over Japan as itinerant English teachers while at the same time preaching the Gospel. Ultimately, they settled in Sendai in Northern Japan and set up their little community. The group found that many Japanese wanted to learn English, and over time, their knowledge of how to teach English became very proficient, so much so that the by-then-expanded community opened a couple of schools to teach English as a foreign language. By the time I got involved in 2014, their English language program—at this point computer-based and using animated characters—seemed to significantly accelerate the learning of English. It was time to take the program international. I was approached by an old friend and prior client, Bud Keilani, who was already working with the group, to develop a tax structure that would work internationally, whether for licensing the IP that had been created or for establishing schools or at least English curriculums that could be expanded to Europe, the US, and beyond.

I was invited to Japan to explain how different types of tax structures might be appropriate. My hosts were two Japanese descendants of the original seven soldiers who, to my great surprise, looked like American football players from the Midwest. They were inordinately hospitable, provided me with guides to explore Tokyo, Sendai, and even the site of Fukushima. I was invited to participate as both observer and speaker at their "town meeting prayer" sessions and literally treated as a member of the family. In fact, we put together a complex plan which would have worked on an international scale, but then disaster hit: the group had planned a film of the life of Christ, to be shot in New Zealand with a set designed to duplicate the ancient city of Jerusalem, and had sunk over $40 million into the project. This created unbelievable strain inside the community and my two hosts—who were on the business side, not the missionary side—bore the brunt of the criticism.

Ultimately, the film was canceled, the international expansion was canceled as well, and the community returned to the insularity of a Japan-based missionary world, sending missionaries throughout Asia and running two schools for teaching English. My friend, Bud, and I were not-so-gently relieved of our responsibilities, and I never did find out what happened to probably the best method of teaching English that had ever been created.

Miss Greece Comes to the Office

The first client I ever had when I opened up my own practice was a former Miss Greece, a statuesque beauty with flowing black hair, part Greek, part French. She called me up and said she had been referred to me by an old friend. Here was her problem: she was earning over a thousand pounds a week in cash in many different currencies, and she was concerned about the then-existing exchange-control rules and the tax liability on the income. I explained the rules to her, and when we finished our meeting, she asked me what my legal fee was. I told her that it was one hundred and fifty pounds. (You can tell by the number that it was a *long* time ago—1974). She looked at me with a coquettish smile and said, "Well, do you want that in cash or kind?" Making one of the few mistakes in my long career, I answered, "I'll take the cash!"

Visiting St. Catherine's Monastery

I represented a number of major Greek families, many of whom arose from the exodus of the Greek shipping community from the US after the Kennedy Tax Act of 1962, which would have taxed Greek (and other) shipowners who were US residents or citizens on their shipping income earned through offshore companies. On one occasion, my wife and I were invited down to the Peloponnese for a weekend to stay in the beautiful family compound of a Greek client. The matriarch of the family and I had business to discuss, but I was also told by her that we should keep ourselves free on that Sunday because she had something special planned. I had no idea what it was. Then Sunday morning came and we boarded the family's helicopter and flew to Athens, where we picked up a private aircraft. We were joined at the airport by a very senior member of the Greek Orthodox Church. Still, I didn't know the purpose of our outing. Then we took off from Athens and flew into Egypt, to the Sinai Desert, and to St. Catherine's Monastery.

Established in 565 AD by Justinian, St. Catherine's is the oldest Eastern Orthodox Christian monastery. It also contains the longest continuously running library of Christianity. At some point in the distant past, the Greek Orthodox Church was given the responsibility for running the monastery. Set at the base of three mountains—one of which is Mount

Sinai—it *feels* ancient. I, myself, had been to St. Catherine's twenty years before when it was a ramshackle monastery that needed serious work. The monastic parties in charge of operating St. Catherine's had cut a deal with the Metropolitan Museum of New York which provided that if the monastery would allow for the museum to exhibit their collection of relics, icons, and manuscripts—considered one of the world's largest collections—the museum would finance a renovation. Which they did. In short time, I would have the pleasure of having seen St. Catherine's before *and* after it had been updated.

But in order to get out of the airport and on to the monastery, we had to go through customs and immigration. The airport at St. Catherine's had been built by the Israeli military during the period in which they had occupied the Sinai (before they had negotiated with Egypt to give it back). Obviously, it was not a commercial airport. In order to get through customs and immigration, the Egyptian government had to send a couple of officials up from Sharm el-Sheikh—by plane, that is, with all expenses paid by us—to provide our group with clearance to enter the country through the military airport and go on into St. Catherine's Monastery. But the arrangements were made, the papers signed, passports stamped, and we were free to enter.

We were greeted at St. Catherine's by a Greek Orthodox monk, fully bearded and in black dress. To my great bewilderment, he spoke English like a Texan. I asked him why, and he told me that he was an American who had attended divinity school in the United States. In the course of doing so, he had become fascinated by the Greek Orthodox Church and taken it upon himself to fly to St. Catherine's and speak with the patriarch and explain to him that he wanted to join the Greek Orthodox Church. He was met with shock. But he assured the patriarch that he meant it. Asked if he was willing to make all the requisite sacrifices, including getting up at four-thirty every morning and praying, he said that yes, he understood the drill. And so, the patriarch took in this divinity-school graduate with the Texan accent. Despite his American origins, he could talk about the history of the Greek Orthodox Church at St. Catherine's Monastery for the last one thousand years with great expertise. For me, this was surprising in the extreme.

We spent the day at St. Catherine's, then flew back to Athens, after which my wife and I went on to London. What a truly extraordinary experience.

My Moustache

In traveling with my first wife to Morocco in 1967, I grew a moustache to blend in with the scenery. I decided that I liked it enough that I would keep it. Eventually, its length developed so much that it became floppy, and I was accused by some of looking like Frank Zappa. I nonetheless kept the moustache.

In 1979, my wife, Dominique, told me that she would like to see what I looked like with a beard, and I replied that, no, I had no intention of growing a beard, that that made no sense to me. But she said that I really should give it a try, and ultimately,

I relented, though with one caveat: the first time someone told me I looked like a rabbi, the beard came off.

The beard remained for nine months. Very conveniently at that point, someone said that I reminded them of a rabbi, and I shaved down to just a moustache right as I was negotiating the final pieces to my deal with Morgan, Lewis & Bockius and had to meet all the senior lawyers at that "white shoe" conservative firm.

I carried that moustache for a few years, until an invitation to a costume party held by my close friends, Rick and Odile Grogan, where everyone had to come dressed up as either a famous or infamous couple. Dominique and I chose to come dressed as Nehru, the first PM of India, and Lady Mountbatten, the wife of Lord Mountbatten, the last viceroy of India. Nehru, of course, is well-known as having had a notorious affair with Lady Mountbatten (and I guess that qualified us as an "infamous couple"). We acquired the costumes from one of my clients, Judith de Paul, an ex-opera singer with the Met who had become a film producer living in London and had done a mini-series entitled *Lord Mountbatten: The Last Viceroy*, which was a very well-recognized documentary. She gave us the use of the costumes that she had brought in for the series so that my wife, statuesque and beautiful, was ready to attend the party with a diamond tiara and long flowing robes. She looked quite stunning. I was done up in a gold Nehru costume. However, when I came down the stairs ready to leave our home for that evening's festivities, my wife reminded me that Nehru did *not* have a moustache. Seeing her point, I promptly went back up the stairs and shaved off the moustache that I had worn for nearly twenty years. We went to the party, and our costumes were no doubt one of the hits of the evening. But hardly anyone recognized that I had taken off my moustache.

From that day in 1983 forward, I kept my face cleanly shaven. That is, until the COVID-19 pandemic, when I reconstituted my bearded face. By that time, the hair was very white, the equivalent of a Wolf Blitzer beard, and that is what I carry to this day.

Morgan Lewis & Park Dilks

In the latter part of 1980, with my boutique practice running along smoothly, I was approached by a lawyer, H. Franklin Bloomer, of Morgan, Lewis & Bockius, about helping the large US firm expand into London and all of Europe. Though Morgan Lewis had tried to do the same a couple of years earlier with an office in Paris, those efforts had failed. Nonetheless, Morgan Lewis still knew they had to go international. After all, they were one of the biggest firms in the US and they had no international office. Franklin Bloomer took me for a very decent lunch, made his pitch for Morgan Lewis wanting to set up in London, and asked whether I would be interested. I said that I would not be, no. I had my successful boutique tax practice, and I could see no reason to merge my firm with theirs. But then Franklin was clever. He said that he understood my position, but to do him a favor: the next time I was in the States, I should call him so that he could introduce me to some of the people at Morgan Lewis. That turned out to be very prophetic. I just so happened to be planning a trip to New York not long thereafter, during which time I would meet one of the most senior partners at Morgan Lewis, Park Dilks. Dilks was a true internationalist, committed to Europe, and he wanted to do something substantial in London.

Next, I met the youngest managing partner in the history of Morgan Lewis, Howard Shecter, a dynamite corporate transaction lawyer out of Philadelphia. And finally, while out in California, I met the head of the office there, Mike Klowden, a corporate transaction lawyer, himself, who had built up a substantial operation in Los Angeles. After being introduced to these three people at the firm—in particular, Howard Shecter, who I met on the eve of the 1980 US presidential election and took to an event at the American Embassy to witness the election results—I changed my mind. I found each of their personalities and commitments to internationalizing the firm quite compelling. And then they all had the same theme: each thought it would be great if I were to run a London office for Morgan Lewis. I, too, now thought so. On March 1, 1981, I merged my practice with Morgan Lewis and opened up their London office, a fairly major event, as not that many of the big US firms had operating practices overseas at that time.

One major issue arose, however: among those people working in my practice, who would come with me? Morgan Lewis refused to make my junior partner, Howard Youngstein, a partner at Morgan Lewis. For some reason, they decided that Howard would not fit into the firm. Morgan Lewis was very firm on this. For them, it was not a question of his abilities as a lawyer. It was a personality issue that they detected, one which led them to conclude that he would not make it into the partnership at Morgan Lewis. Howard never forgave me for going ahead with the plan anyway. Whether he thought I should not have taken advantage of the opportunity and stayed with him, I don't know. At the same time, I thought my senior associate, whom I had brought over from the US, a first-class young tax lawyer, Jeffrey Gould, would come with me and that the corporate associate, Philip Weinrich, would go with Howard if he wanted to set up his own firm. But I was wrong. The senior associate chose not to go with me but went with Howard instead. That was a real shock, and it reminded me of what had happened to my own father when he broke up his partnership with a small number of lawyers some thirty years before.

My father was a very fine lawyer and well regarded in Washington, and there was a junior associate that he assumed would go with him who changed his mind at the last minute and decided to go with my father's much-less-talented but very affable younger partner. Why did he go? Because he thought he could dominate that new partnership—and he was correct. Rather than stay in my father's shadow—as my father had likewise started his own firm—he opted to go out on his own. In his case, he was correct. He ended up dominating the other lawyer and eventually built up his own firm which became very prominent in DC. Although I was personally hurt by the fact that the tax associate did not want to join me, I understood his decision. Sure enough, he set up a firm with Howard Youngstein, and it worked out very well for Jeffrey.

In March 1981, I joined Morgan Lewis as their first lawyer outside the United States in what was called their International Section, an invention of Park Dilks, consisting of those lawyers with international work. I had never been at a major law firm. I wouldn't say I was intimidated by the strength and power of the major US law firms and their amazing talent, but I had my apprehensions, for I had had something of an eclectic legal life up to that point practicing tax law. I knew the IRS, had done some interesting work at my father's old firm, began learning UK tax law at Margulies and Sterling, not to mention all I had learned while running my own practice. But joining one of the top firms in the US at a senior level was a big step for me, and it took a while before I became confident in the delivery of services, as well as working with the various lawyers that made up the practice.

And how was I performing at my job? Indeed, what *did* Morgan Lewis think of me?

Park Dilks took responsibility for the London office, and some six months into the firm's experiment in the international arena, he was invited to speak to the Management Committee about how things were coming along, including matters concerning billing, collection, clients, *and* me. Park went into the Management Committee and said, "Gentlemen, here's my report. When we set up the London office, we sent Joe Hennessy as a helper to Chuck in developing the office." Joe was an experienced corporate transactions partner who knew everyone in the Philadelphia office and throughout the firm and was a great help in assisting me in the resource choices that were required. "His job was to stamp Morgan, Lewis & Bockius on Chuck's independent forehead. Chuck's job was to get Joe Hennessy laid. Chuck failed. Hennessy succeeded. End of report."

That became an apocryphal story in the lineage of Morgan Lewis, and Park repeated that story at his own retirement party for the partners. It was hysterically funny. I suppose I was doing just fine at my new position at Morgan Lewis.

After Park retired, I was given the chairmanship of the International Section, which took my attention to places beyond London as we set up offices in Belgium, Paris, and Frankfurt and looked carefully at what we would do in the Far East. Park's pet project finally ended when the International Section eventually disbanded into three sections, including regulatory, corporate transactions, and tax law. I joined the tax section and remained there until I finally retired at seventy-four, in October of 2015.

One of the most enjoyable experiences of my long association with Morgan Lewis was my participation with the "Morgan Lewis Players" in the musical performance at our annual Partners Meeting. Written primarily and directed by New York partner Stuart Sarnoff, the performance was essentially a spoof on many designated partners, executed with enough cleverness and caustic humor as to be worthy of an off-Broadway show. In fact, we had a Broadway session-musician ensemble to help. Over the years that I was involved, I had the honor of being the opening act, charged with loosening up the crowd and preparing them for the humorous invective that was to follow. Each year I delivered one or two classic rock or blues songs, including "Roll Over Beethoven," "Jailhouse Rock," and "Blue Suede Shoes": vintage rock from a then-vintage partner.

The Columbus Group

In 1979, I had a handful of friends who were successful, practicing tax lawyers, all of us about the same age, in our mid-to-late thirties, and friends of or known to one another. The six of us thought it would be exciting to get together in a different part of the world and talk about the tax law. The group consisted of John Van Merkensteijn, a partner at the time with his own firm; Perry Lerner, a partner from O'Melveny and Myers; Bill Gifford, a partner at Davis Polk; Bill McKee, soon to become the tax legislative counsel of the US Treasury; and Peter Whiteman, eminent international tax barrister and the youngest Queen's Counsel in recent memory. We were all, in our own way, leading young international tax lawyers in our rarified world. Together for a long weekend each year, we did a lot of complex tax-problem solving, with each of us presenting an interesting or complicated problem that we had faced in the preceding year, discussing it over a several-hour session, often heated but always insightful, to be followed by a two-or-three-star Michelin meal at the hotel where we were staying or in the regions we were visiting.

Our sojourns included Saint-Germain-en-Laye, outside Paris; San Francisco; Kiawah Island, South Carolina; the Loire Valley in France; Venice; Budapest; the South of France; Sicily; Istanbul; and a number of other wonderful venues. This program lasted for a long time, and resolved (at least in our own minds) some extremely complicated problems. I will not discuss any of them here, as some were criminal cases, or aggressive tax shelters, or just complicated problems that could go in one of several different directions. But it was on balance a brilliant experience that went on for close to twenty years. We did lose one member, but the remaining five of us carried on for the duration. In fairness, over time as we all became more experienced and needed less help from other talented young tax lawyers to solve our problems, the group which had started with these long, descriptive three-to-four-hour presentations, became solely committed to golf, drinking, or eating; and the amount of time committed to the tax law shrunk considerably, down to an hour or so. But professionally, this was one of the best legal experiences I ever had, and I believe I can say that the same is true for the rest of the group.

We've remained friends throughout all these years, despite no longer meeting up with one another for intellectual stimulation or extraordinary cuisine.

CHAPTER NINE

An Economic Benedict Arnold: on Expatriation

In the early years of my London practice, I encountered a significant number of American citizens who seriously questioned whether they wanted to remain American or if they were better off expatriating. There were, of course, a few Americans who wanted to expatriate for political reasons. In most cases, however, taxation was at issue. The United States taxes its citizens on their worldwide income and their worldwide estate when they die. For many Americans already living abroad, especially those with no plans of returning to the US, questions of expatriation often arose. I was always happy to help these clients. In fact, at my first little boutique firm and my early years at Morgan Lewis, we expatriated more people than almost any other law firm in London. Some individuals, including a few lawyers, critical of my willingness to do so, branded me an "economic Benedict Arnold." But more on that later.

In the 1970s, it was relatively easy to give up one's citizenship. One could do so by going before a consular officer at a US Embassy and filing the application for expatriation. First, the individual had to prove that he had a second citizenship, as the US does not allow an American to give up citizenship and become stateless. Statements were then made to the consular officer about the desire to give up one's citizenship. Interestingly, consular officers would often intervene and try to dissuade the expatriating party. They would say, "Why would you ever want to give up your American citizenship? You must be crazy. You're thinking incorrectly." In fact, consular officers even had the ability to say that an applicant must first go through a "cooling off" period of some thirty days. In any event, I had my share of people who had already thought hard about whether to expatriate and had concluded that it was indeed the right decision.

Because an American looking to expatriate had to have an alternative citizenship, some of my clients needed new citizenships in foreign countries. A whole body of law exists in different jurisdictions about how a person could acquire citizenship. In some countries, for instance, one could purchase a citizenship with ease. In parts of the Caribbean, like St. Kitts and Nevis, one could buy a property for a few hundred thousand dollars and then spend a bit of time as a legitimate resident on the island, and citizenship was granted. Also, in the early-to-mid-1970s, Ireland offered an opportunity for citizenship. If a person made a significant contribution to the Irish economy by making an investment of about £250,000 or bought a substantial property in the country, Irish citizenship could be granted. One of the earliest expatriations I had involved a Chinese American client that lived in San Francisco, earned significant income outside the US, and wanted to expatriate. The head of the family was living in London, had no desire to spend time in the US, and her assets were mostly abroad. So, we got her Irish citizenship. We also got Irish citizenship for a client who was setting up a major hedge-fund operation and anticipated earning significant income outside the United States. He moved to Bermuda, ran a billion-dollar hedge fund, made a lot of money on his own, and after several years of work and time spent in Bermuda (and *not* in the United States), he and his wife decided that they had had enough and wanted to return to the US. The US welcomed back people who had expatriated. Naturally, my client and anyone else in such a circumstance had to go through the full application process: first, applying for a work visa (this client had his hedge fund in the United States and so that wasn't a problem); then applying for a green card to live as a permanent resident of the United States; and then, after having this green card for several years, applying for citizenship. My client did this with my assistance and was granted US citizenship for a second time. Therefore, after giving up one's citizenship of the United States, the opportunity to get it back *could* be there for those who would like to reacquire it.

Within the realm of expatriation, it is important to know and understand the term "accidental American." I have expatriated many in my day. But then what is an "accidental American?" Let's take a case I had of a Belgian who had moved to the United States to work for an international organization. After a few years in the US, he and his wife returned to Belgium. But in the interim, they had had a child, and that child, by virtue of having been born in the US, was an American citizen. Down the line, this could be a tremendous advantage; many people would love to have American citizenship. But if the family was of substance and came from a country outside the US, it could be a real disadvantage. For instance, I had a client from one of the leading industrial families in Europe whose son was married to a US citizen. Unfortunately, the son died, leaving behind a three-year-old child, and then the patriarch himself became very ill and passed away. Under the rules of the Napoleonic Code in existence for two centuries throughout Europe, when the patriarch died, a good portion of his estate passed onto the lineal descendants, in this case, bypassing the wife of the deceased son and going down to the three-year-old. Now, this child had no relationship to the United States. He didn't live there; his mother was born in the US, and this made him a citizen of that country. That was it. So then should the child have to pay a hefty tax on the non-US income of his substantial inheritance to the United States Treasury? My client did not think so. Therefore, I faced the question of whether it was possible to expatriate a three-year-old on the theory that the parents were the guardians and the child would have the right to reverse the citizenship when he was eighteen and no longer a minor. As much as I tried, I failed. The American embassy said that one could not expatriate a child of three. So we acquiesced and solved the problem that came from being an "accidental American" by diverting the inheritance in such a way that it came to him when he was old enough to expatriate on his own.

Sometimes the circumstances around expatriation are far more quaint, even entertaining. Consider the case of the seventh earl of Cowley, who became the seventh earl of Cowley in 1975 after his nephew, the sixth earl of Cowley, died. With the passing of his nephew, he was in a position to join the House of Lords. But, as an American, he was afraid that by joining the House of Lords he would have to forfeit his American citizenship under the then-existing US statutory law. We did everything we could to get him to keep his American citizenship. We had him swear out an affidavit to the consular officer in London in which he said he was born in America, that he loved America, that he had served in the American Armed Services, but that he had been given an opportunity with the death of his nephew to join the House of Lords and that he also loved his lineage in England, and that ultimately he would like to honor that lineage *and* remain an American. We swore out that affidavit in the morning and he was invested into the House of Lords in the afternoon.

Our argument stemmed from a recent Supreme Court decision which stated that one did not lose American citizenship automatically by doing an "expatriating act" such as taking an oath of allegiance to a foreign power, serving in a foreign government, or acquiring a second citizenship unless, in doing so, one intended to give up that American citizenship. This Supreme Court decision concluded that American citizenship was a right, not a privilege granted by the government that could be easily withdrawn. This was an unusual situation where a client wanted to retain American citizenship by doing an expatriating act, that is, serving in a foreign government, and we found a solution without a US or UK tax burden.

In the mid-to-late 1990s, we did many expatriations, including The Right Honourable Yehudi Menuhin, many "accidental Americans" and a number of Americans who expatriated solely for tax avoidance purposes. Some expatriations (not ours) were perceived to be abusive, and the Press had a field day in attacking these "economic Benedict Arnolds." For example, a prominent American businessman who owned a substantial property in Florida took citizenship in a Caribbean jurisdiction, expatriated, and came back to the same house in Florida as a cultural attaché from the jurisdiction of which he now had citizenship. That diplomatic status granted him diplomatic immunity which included no US tax liabilities. Congress soon intervened. As part of an Immigration Reform Act passed in 1996, Senator Jack Reed proposed an amendment to the Act ("the Reed Amendment") that said that entry to the US could be denied to persons who had renounced their US citizenship for tax avoidance purposes. This law is still in effect, although it has very rarely been implemented. On the other hand, over the next ten years, Congress passed tax legislation that significantly constrained the ability to freely expatriate with no tax consequences, culminating in very stringent legislation in 2008 that drastically reduced the number of Americans who would expatriate.

Americans abroad weighing the benefits and burdens of expatriation did not anticipate such tough legislation. Two harsh results came of it: one, a US citizen who had more than $2 million in net worth or who paid an average net income tax over the preceding five years of $124,000 (adjusted for inflation) would be deemed to sell his worldwide assets and had to pay capital gains taxes on the appreciation of all his assets (with an exemption of $600,000—also adjusted for inflation). There was a narrow exception for dual citizens at birth. And two, if a so-called "covered expatriate" made gifts to a US citizen (such as a child, though not a spouse), the gifts were not treated as gifts but were taxable income to the US citizen recipient.

For Americans abroad, these harsh expatriation laws are the price of having a tax system based on citizenship and not residency or domicile. It now makes expatriation a potentially expensive privilege. Many say they don't care and will pay the freight. I continue to have clients who seek help in considering expatriation. Personally, I feel that if a person wants to give up his American citizenship, if he feels he doesn't belong in America, he/she should be able to do so without such a significant financial burden. Many lawyers, however, have been critical of me for helping Americans expatriate. Some, as noted, have even referred to me as an economic Benedict Arnold. And yet, I don't think helping an individual expatriate from the US makes me a bad person. Rather, I would say it makes me a good lawyer.

As for me, after over fifty years living in London, readers may wonder whether I, myself, ever expatriated. The answer is no, for after the laws were changed in 2008, I couldn't afford to expatriate. I pay tax on my worldwide income to both the US and the UK governments. There are reciprocal credits in doing so, as one is not supposed to be subject to double taxation. But that's a complicated arena. Anyone in such a situation would need a good tax lawyer to weave through the complexities.

CHAPTER TEN
Risk/Reward

Notwithstanding all these unusual and interesting stories I have told you involving so many exceptional personages, many in the entertainment industry, my practice in fact was significantly broader and more orthodox than these storylines. My initial US tax practice expanded over all these years and morphed into one that represented individuals, families, and family businesses, almost always with a cross-border element. I didn't exclusively represent Americans. Because I had so much exposure to so many people in my fifty-plus years of practice, I really didn't know from where my next client would come from one day to the next: it could have been the recommendation from a high school friend, an old friend from Yale, someone from law school, or even from my golfing career or from the myriad of people I met from my life in London. In the early years, I did a significant amount of speaking, writing, and editing on American and international

tax matters, and many clients came from this exposure. There was just no way I could anticipate from
where the next client would come.

I ended up representing a lot of families and
individuals, and sometimes, I acted as a consigliere
to these clients. They trusted my knowledge of
US and later UK tax law; they valued my judgment; they benefitted from using me as a sounding
board or having me choose the right lawyers to go
about solving different problems. After I merged
my practice in 1981 with Morgan Lewis and then
in 2015 joined as senior counsel with McDermott
Will & Emery, I expanded my existing practice
and continued with corporate and tax structuring,
estate tax and trust planning, and individual tax
and personal planning. This covered a vast array
of people from the US, UK, Switzerland, Austria,
Greece, Italy, Lebanon, Saudi Arabia, Egypt, Kenya,
Germany, India, Jordan, Japan, and places beyond.
My practice was an international practice in the
deepest sense, always with a cross-border reference. Indeed, I never had a single client who was
only US *or* only UK. My practice was truly exciting
to me. I didn't know what kind of an opportunity
I might have from one day to the next. As it were,
this is all I can say about this broad-based practice,
for I was acting as a lawyer and there are obvious
client privacy and confidentiality issues that I
would never think of jeopardizing. The fact that
some of my most interesting cases involved major
families—well, those simply will not be discussed as
part of this improbable journey.

One of the most satisfying aspects of my professional life has been my varying contributions to charitable endeavors, most of which relate to providing opportunities to young people in the UK. The earliest of these contributions in my life in the UK was acting as the head of the Alumnae Schools Committee for Yale in London in interviewing students from England and Wales who applied to the university. In the earliest years, applicants were few, maybe twelve to fifteen students a year and mostly from the American School in London. During my years of responsibility in this role (about seventeen years in total) and following in my role as president of the Yale Club of London, the applicant pool massively increased so that today there are more than four hundred applicants to Yale from all over England and Wales; and now the applicant pool consists of about one third American students, one third British students, and one third third-country nationals studying in the UK.

Another of my charitable roles was as a member of the Fulbright Commission in the UK., one of the first of the non-academic business community members that resulted from a meaningful policy change through the cultural attaché at the US embassy, Anne Collins. The initiative resulted in major contributions by the business community in the expansion of the reach of the Fulbright Commission in the UK. I put together three fellowships financed and implemented by my own law firm, Morgan Lewis, and two of my clients, John Cleese and Robert Wise, founder of the Wise Music Group Ltd. All three fellowships provided major opportunities for UK citizens to study in the US in their chosen profession. With Morgan Lewis, we put together a fellowship for a young UK solicitor to study US securities law with part time work in our Washington, DC office. With John Cleese, we provided a fellowship to a US university such as UCLA, USC, or NYU to study screen writing for feature films. Finally, Bob Wise agreed to fund a fellowship sending a young British composer to study music composition at a major US university or music school. These experiences were invaluable to these young people and often resulted in a significant enhancement of their career opportunities.

I also served on the boards of the US Foundation for Kew Gardens, the UK Board of the National Philanthropic Trust, and committees at the National Gallery and the Royal Academy of Arts. One of the most interesting contributions was my development of the fundraising memorial for John Barry with John's widow, Laurie Barry, and the creation with Laurie of a graduate fellowship at the Royal College of Music in composition for film. (See the reference above in Chapter 2.) One fascinating piece of artistic history was my role in negotiation for the renovation of Room 34 at the National Gallery. This was a complete restoration of the room to its nineteenth-century grandeur, which included taking out all of the whitewashed parts in the ceiling, revealing vignettes of the most famous (and not-so-famous) British artists at the time (1876–1877). These were all cleaned up and restored with silk screen printing showing the originals. The one famous British artist that was not included was the satirist of rakes and royalty, William Hogarth, and the Gallery quietly agreed to add him with his own vignette in one of the two unadorned spaces left in the ceiling—and with the current date, 1995.

Now what have I learned from this journey, especially about myself? The extraordinary array of people that crossed my path over my years in London tested out an element in my character that had only been hinted at in my earlier years—that is, a sense of personal democracy in dealing with people. By this I mean a non-judgmental respect for the diverse cultures and people I had been exposed to and a continued curiosity about the different worlds that they represented. This doesn't mean I wasn't critical, but it does mean I started with an open mind. It also means that I could identify and deal with those who felt "entitled" or those who thrived on inequality and knew how to "kiss up and piss down," as the saying goes.

My Kikuyu partner in Kenya, for example, had been in detention as a Mau Mau in the Kikuyu uprising against the British, yet he went on to get his PhD in political science some years after Kenyan independence. I trusted him completely as a business partner. Marilyn Chambers may have been a hardcore pornography star, but she was also a fine off-Broadway actress and a respectable and appreciative client. My evangelical Japanese clients may have had a belief system and practices that I really could not comprehend, but they were deferential to those with differing belief systems, listened carefully as clients, and were thoughtful in their responses. Without that sense of personal democracy and a good "listening" ear, I seriously doubt I could have succeeded in building my unique and varied client world. Sometimes, however, my willingness to listen and show initial respect for some pretty fanciful and hairbrained ideas led inevitably to much wastage of time, though occasionally some friendships and even a successful client or two.

Another quality which I developed in my practice was a willingness to take on small matters with a reasonable hope that they could either turn into large matters or expose me to people who would become clients or friends. This included, as indicated in my stories, a very small matter for the then-US Muppets and a one-off concert appearance for Michael Jackson. It also included, for example, representation of a start-up perfume business in London and Paris led by a very smooth but unsavory ex-perfumier. Though the business went into bankruptcy in both London and Paris, I made many long friendships and developed a number of clients among the suffering investors.

In retrospect, the most surprising thing I learned about myself was my capacity for taking risks. As discussed in my departure from the IRS, all my contemporaries thought that I was a total nut case to do what I was doing—that is, stopping a clear career path and moving to Africa. But the fact of the matter is, I did evaluate the risks in terms of what I could afford to do financially and for how long I was prepared to commit to a new path. I didn't run off to Kenya shooting crap. I had some money that I had inherited with the passing of my father. This would seem to be a good way to use a portion of it to cover my cost of living for a couple of years to see where this venture might lead. And that is exactly what it did. Likewise, instead of setting up my own practice in London, I could have gone back to the US to join a US law firm. But again, I had enough money saved that I was willing to take the risk of setting up my own practice as a sole practitioner in a part of the world that I had not grown up in and barely knew.

Again, evaluating the risks was an important piece of ultimately taking those steps. With that said, however, my leaps into the unknown, from Communist Russia, to Kenya, to London, to East Germany, to Liechtenstein, to the Netherlands Antilles, and the Seychelles and Mauritius with my dear "coke dinner" date—all of these ventures required faith in the benefits of risk and the belief that without risk there can be no great rewards. Brought back to Harvard Law School in 2000 to speak at the Traphagen Distinguished Alumni Speaker Series, I hoped to impress as much on those students seated before me that day. Perhaps I was able to reach some of them, and perhaps, with my *Improbable Journey*, I have been able to do the same here with you.

BIBLIOGRAPHICAL NOTES

1. Edward Rothstein, "CONCERT: A FESTIVAL OF HUMMEL," *The New York Times,* May 3, 1982, https://www.nytimes.com/1982/05/03/arts/concert-a-festival-of-hummel.html.

2. The Hummel Project, Orpheus & Bacchus, 2009.

3. Johann Nepomuk Hummel, *A Complete Theoretical and Practical Course of Instruction on the Art of Playing the Piano Forte* (London, 1829).

4. Hogan, Michael, "The Englishman Behind the Muppets," *London Daily Telegraph*, August 1, 2020, https://www.telegraph.co.uk/tv/2020/07/30/muppet-man-lew-grade-invented-popular-tv/.

5. D. W. McKim and Phillip Chapman, "Kris Kristofferson and Rita Coolidge – Episode 49," Muppetcentral.com, https://muppetcentral.com/guides/episodes/tms/season3/49_kristofferson_coolidge.shtml.

6. Mel Goldberg and Marilyn Chambers, *Sex Surrogate*, Las Vegas, 1979, https://www.amazon.com/

215

Surrogate-MARILYN-CHAMBERS-Woman-Show/
dp/B07CWJG38H.

7. Rebecca Cope, "The true story of the Duchess of
Argyll, one-time *Tatler* columnist and the 'dirty
duchess' at the heart of *A Very British Scandal*,"
Tatler.com, December 24, 2021, https://www.tatler.
com/gallery/gallery-margaret-of-argyll.

8. Alyce Faye Eichelberger Cleese, *Alyce in Maurice-
land.*

9. *Norman v. Times Newspapers*, December 11, 2000.

10. Robert Hilburn, "The long and winding road," *The
Los Angeles Times*, September 22, 1985, https://
www.latimes.com/la-et-hilburn-michael-jackson-
sep22-story.html.

ACKNOWLEDGMENTS

There are numerous people to whom I am indebted in making contributions to my life story, including the collection of stories related in this book. I have, however, limited the acknowledgments herein to those persons who either pushed me or inspired me to write this *Improbable Journey* or who willingly or unwittingly aided significantly to the storytelling or the tax insights that resulted in this book. Many of these contributors are already acknowledged in various sections of the book, so I will try not to duplicate the references.

There are two specific people who "pushed" me or inspired me to write this tale: Gilbert Harrison and Philippe Labro. Gilbert is one of my oldest friends from the days of Camp Robin Hood whom my wife, Dominique, and I met on a beach in Nantucket over forty years ago. We, along with his wife, Shelley, have been friends since that chance meeting on the beach. Gilbert has written his own autobiography, *Deal Junkie*, on his fascinating life in the retail and fashion industry. He simply said, "You have to write your story. Your stories are more interesting than mine!" He suggested Post Hill Press as an appropriate publisher and JT as a person who could help shape the narrative to make it digestible and exciting for a readership. And it all came to pass! Philippe Labro is a prominent French author, journalist, film director, and television host; and he and his wife, Francoise, have been friends of my wife and I for many years. We have holidayed together summer and winter in Gstaad, Switzerland. On hearing my stories, especially from the entertainment industry, as well as my unusual sojourn in post-independence Kenya, he implored me to simply sit down and dictate, bit by bit in a James Joycian sort of way, my collection of stories as a stream of consciousness that eventually could be shaped into a life's journey in writing. I resisted each year, and he would ask me the next year if I had started. Whether this was a push or an inspiration I really don't know, but eventually I relented and delivered. I guess it helped that he has written twenty-four books, fiction and non-fiction, so he did know what he was talking about.

I have to give a meaningful acknowledgement to my father, Nathan Lubar, who, as detailed more fully in the text, was an extraordinary role model who directed me ever so gently to study both the law and taxation as something that would be valuable no matter what I ended up doing with my life. But after my father died and I had graduated from law school, the person who really gave me direction was Al Arent, founding and then-senior partner of a venerable Washington law firm, Arent Fox. I knew Al from the golf course, as a family friend and an executor of my father's estate. He is the one who said to me that if I wanted to be a tax lawyer, I should work in the government first and preferably the Chief Counsel's Office of the IRS. That's what I did, and the rest really is history.

Then there were the entrepreneurial lawyers Barry Sterling and Irwin Margulies, the two US lawyers in London who "hired me off the streets" in my first exposure to legal life in London. Without their belief in me, I would probably have gone home to Washington, DC, and no matter what I did, it would not have been comparable to the extraordinary life I have led. As detailed in the text, I left Margulies & Sterling and set up my own firm. I was inordinately helped in this endeavor and in my subsequent life at Morgan Lewis by my longtime secretary and PA, Moira D'Olivera, who for most of my career was with me longer than each wife—Dominique eventually caught up. Moira really ran my legal life. She knew my entire client list, and they knew her. She mastered technology as it developed for the law, ran my client files and personal files, and was indispensable to my career, building my own practice, merging my practice with Morgan Lewis, and carrying on there for thirty-four years. I miss her to this day.

In building my own practice, I have to give credit to the younger partner I brought into my practice, Howard Youngstein. Although not trained as a tax lawyer, he was very helpful in building our boutique international practice. I was very sorry that Morgan Lewis would not bring him into the merged practice.

I merged my practice in 1981 with Morgan Lewis, and in those early years, I was helped enormously by Joe Hennessy, a corporate partner in Philadelphia, who really integrated me with Morgan Lewis (see Chapter 8). In addition, I brought into the fledgling London office Joan Ingram, a US-trained lawyer who was committed to London and had both a first-class legal mind and a commitment to practice that is something of a rarity in today's world. Early on, I could rely on Joan to handle a wide variety of matters, many of which she had not had exposure to until she joined our practice. Moreover, inside the first five years she was with me, she had three daughters but was still able to carry on the practice and motherhood at the same time. I was very sorry she decided to retire when I finally left Morgan Lewis.

In addition to Joe and Joan, I had a lot of help from Michael Pfeifer. Hired as an associate, he was the first lawyer at Morgan Lewis who moved from associate into partnership outside the United States. He was a fine tax lawyer, but unfortunately, he insisted on returning to the US when he separated from his first wife who had moved to the US with their young children. Michael went on to an excellent career with Ernst & Young, the IRS, and then with a prominent Washington D.C. firm, Caplin & Drysdale.

Without question, I am indebted to the senior management of Morgan Lewis, including the three partners I first interviewed with—that is, Park Dilks,

Howard Shecter, and Mike Klowden. All three gave me significant support through the merger process, continued to support me in the growth of the London office, and have remained good friends to this day; although Park unfortunately died not long after he retired from the firm some thirty years ago. Likewise, I benefited from the exceptional talents of the lawyers in the firm, especially in the tax section and the personal law section. Most of the stories in the book either continued on after my merger with Morgan Lewis or originated while I was a partner with the firm. I would also like to thank the senior management of McDermott Will & Emery, especially the London office, which brought me into the firm at seventy-four after I retired from Morgan Lewis.

And then there is my immediate family. I am convinced that many of my clients over the years stayed with me partly through the charm, hospitality, and engaging personality of my wife, Dominique, as best illustrated by my oft-stated comment that "clients became friends and friends became clients," and I usually can't remember who started as one or the other. Then there were my son, Alex, my daughter, Katherine, and my stepson, Pascal, each of whom in his/her own way provided emotional support, wisdom from their own lives, companionship, and lots of fun over all these years. I think the most apt comment came from Alex in his words written in The Book of Chuck created by all three of them for my eightieth birthday celebration: "The Old Man has always led by example, which of course if you know him can cut a couple of ways.

Rather than tell me, he showed me that hard work, transparency, good humor and well-timed naps can take you far in life. Listen just enough that you feel genuine empathy for others, follow just enough that you learn from those around you and sprinkle in just enough contrarianism that your path is your very own."

And finally, a warm thank you to Debra Englander and her compatriots at Post Hill Press, including Heather King, who believed that my improbable journey was worth describing in print!

ABOUT THE AUTHOR

Charles Lubar is a graduate of Yale University and Harvard Law School and holds a Master's Degree in taxation from Georgetown Law. For two-and-a-half years he worked in the Chief Counsel's Office of the Internal Revenue Service in Washington, D.C. He spent thirty-four years as a partner for the global law firm Morgan Lewis. Lubar most recently served as a Senior Counsel at McDermott Will & Emery. Born and raised in Washington, D.C., Lubar spent two years as an entrepreneur in Nairobi, Kenya and has been a resident of London, England since 1971.